WHAT PRINCIPALS NEED TO KNOW ABOUT

Teaching and Learning Writing

RUTH CULHAM

A Joint Publication

 Solution Tree

 SCHOLASTIC

 naesp

555 North Morton Street
Bloomington, IN 47404
800.733.6786 (toll free) / 812.336.7700
FAX: 812.336.7790

email: info@solution-tree.com
solution-tree.com

Visit **go.solution-tree.com/leadership** to download the reproducibles in this book.

Printed in the United States of America

17 16 15 14 13   1 2 3 4 5

Library of Congress Cataloging-in-Publication Data

Culham, Ruth.
   What principals need to know about teaching and learning writing / Ruth Culham. -- First edition.
      pages cm
   Includes bibliographical references and index.
   ISBN 978-1-936765-43-0 (perfect bound) 1. English language--Composition and exercises--Study and teaching--Handbooks, manuals, etc. 2. School principals--United States--Handbooks, manuals, etc. I. Title.
   LB1576.C8468 2014
   808'.042071--dc23

Solution Tree
Jeffrey C. Jones, CEO
Edmund M. Ackerman, President

Solution Tree Press
President: Douglas M. Rife
Editorial Director: Lesley Bolton
Managing Production Editor: Caroline Wise
Senior Production Editor: Edward Levy
Copy Editor: Rachel Rosolina
Proofreader: Sarah Payne-Mills
Text Designer: Raven Bongiani
Text Compositor: Rian Anderson
Cover Designer: Amy Shock

For Sam, always

ACKNOWLEDGMENTS

Over the years, I've had the great pleasure to meet and work with many gifted administrators. To each of you, I offer the most sincere appreciation for your dedication to making sure students in your schools can write and write well. Thank you for letting me be your partner in this important work. I've learned right alongside you and your staff every day. What a wonderful journey.

In particular, I'd like to thank the administrators who contributed the quotations at the start of each chapter: Carol Hailey McLean, K–12 reading/language arts resource specialist, Shawnee Mission School District, Johnson County, Kansas; Valerie Truesdale, superintendent, and Jamie Pinckney, principal, Okatie Elementary School, Beaufort County School District, South Carolina; Erin Bailey, instructional coach, Blue Springs School District, Missouri; Gaye Lantz, director of curriculum, American International School of Lagos, Nigeria; John Nittolo, superintendent/principal, Green Hills School, Greendell, New Jersey; and Rhett Boudreau, assistant principal, Mountain View Middle School, Beaverton, Oregon. And to Debbie Morris, principal, Acworth Elementary, Georgia—thank you for your beautiful words about me and the work we've done together. Although they don't appear here, I hold them dear.

Many thanks to the professional book division at Scholastic, especially Virginia Dooley, editor in chief of teaching resources, for graciously allowing me to use many of my core scoring guides and other materials in this text. Since the strength of the work is in common language, I appreciate Scholastic's support as the ideas I developed with them find a new audience here.

Solution Tree Press would like to thank the following reviewers:

Jason Albrecht
Principal
Northwest Elementary School
Ankeny, Iowa

Sheila Aldredge
Principal
William B. Miller Elementary School
Dallas, Texas

Shawn Allen
Principal
Sunland Park Elementary School
Fort Lauderdale, Florida

Michael Behrmann
Principal
North Hill Elementary School
Rochester Hills, Michigan

Michael Curry
Principal
Amesbury Middle School
Amesbury, Massachusetts

Alicia LaFrance
Principal
Pelham Elementary School
Pelham, New Hampshire

Scott Mitchell
Principal
Watergrass Elementary School
Wesley Chapel, Florida

Tonika Peavy
Principal
South Plaquemines Elementary School
Port Sulphur, Louisiana

Paula Reber
Principal
Linntown Intermediate School
Lewisburg, Pennsylvania

Jacque Shayne
Principal
Mount Scott Elementary School
Happy Valley, Oregon

TABLE OF CONTENTS

Visit **go.solution-tree.com/leadership** to download the reproducibles in this book.

Reproducible pages are in italics.

FIVE

SIX

ABOUT THE AUTHOR

 **Ruth Culham, EdD,** is the president of the Culham Writing Company and former unit manager of the Assessment Program at Education Northwest in Portland, Oregon. Ruth was English Teacher of the Year in Montana, the highlight of her nineteen-year teaching career. She holds specialty degrees in library science and elementary, middle, and secondary English education.

As a pioneering researcher in writing assessment and instruction, Ruth creates and conducts teacher workshops to provide professional development at local, district, and state levels. At state and national conferences, she's a featured speaker on using traits of writing, designing effective writing instruction, reading to teach writing, and other related topics.

Ruth is the recognized expert in the "traits of writing" field and has authored over forty teaching resources published by Scholastic, including *6+1 Traits of Writing: The Complete Guide, Grades 3 and Up*; *6+1 Traits of Writing: The Complete Guide for the Primary Grades*; and *Traits of Writing: The Complete Guide for Middle School*, which was the winner of *Learning Magazine*'s 2011 Teachers' Choice award. As the author of *Traits Writing: The Complete K–8 Writing Program* (2012), she has launched a writing revolution. *Traits Writing* is the culmination of forty years of educational experience, research, practice, and passion.

INTRODUCTION

For nineteen years, I taught in schools with principals who had a variety of skills and beliefs. What I noticed was this: When the principal was a good communicator, ran efficient meetings, and took care of details large and small, I had a successful year, and my students thrived. But when the principal shied away from discussions, didn't return emails or schedule meetings, and lacked follow-through, it was much more stressful, and I didn't accomplish nearly what I had planned.

Since leaving the classroom and becoming an advocate for high-quality writing assessment and instruction, I've learned that the principal can make or break a school. He or she quite literally manages the equivalent of a small city—both people and facilities. The principal handles schedules, staff, curriculum, staff development, compliance, meetings, parents, and, yes, in many cases, bus and lunchroom duty. Those who possess or develop a vision of what their school should and could become, succeed. Those who are mired in day-to-day operations and politics, don't.

It is with great appreciation for everything that principals do that I offer you this book about assessing and teaching writing and optimizing the learning environment for every student writer in your school. Whether you are the principal of a large urban, a medium-sized suburban, or a small rural school, the same ideas will work. But principals are not the only audience for this book: curriculum directors, literacy coaches, and anyone helping to improve the school writing program will find it useful.

Teachers are hungry for leadership and support in order to make their writing classrooms places where important learning takes place every single day. In this book, I offer ideas I've gathered from schools where, only five minutes in the door, it's clear that writing matters, students are eager to write, and teachers find teaching writing to be one of the best times of the day.

We've made progress in writing instruction over the past decades, but we aren't even close to our goal of every student being a skilled and capable writer. As we enter the era of Common Core State Standards (CCSS), writing has never been more important. In the Carnegie Foundation's report *Informing Writing: The Benefits of Formative Assessment* (Graham, Harris, & Hebert, 2011), we are reminded that teaching writing has social implications beyond the classroom: "Helping these young people learn to write clearly, coherently, and logically will expand their access to higher education, give them the skills needed to be successful at work, and increase the likelihood that they will actively participate as citizens of a literate society" (p. 33).

The stage is set for a new era of writing instruction.

A Brief History of Writing Instruction

To understand why we are where we are today in writing instruction, it's useful to look at its evolution. This abbreviated history looks at the research, the big names, the influences, and the trends over the last half century.

The 1960s

In the early 1960s, the National Council of Teachers of English (NCTE) commissioned a study by prominent researchers Richard Braddock, Richard Lloyd-Jones, and Lowell Schoer (1963) to document the methods used to teach writing in elementary and secondary schools in order to learn which, if any, were effective. The report, *Research in Written Composition*, stated that there was "only a rudimentary understanding of teaching writing" (p. 5) by class-room teachers at all levels. Pointing to a lack of consistent terminology and methodologies, the researchers concluded that "the field as a whole is laced with dreams, prejudices, and make-shift operations" (p. 5). The report also denounced the teaching of isolated grammar skills, noting that, in addition to being ineffective, this time-honored practice thwarted teachers' attempts to show students how to compose for real purposes. This new way of thinking about writing instruction set the stage for a more process-based approach—one that emphasized the creation of the product over the product itself.

The 1970s

The practical reality of shifting the emphasis in instruction from product to process became the focus of study during the 1970s. Researchers Janet Emig (1971) and Sondra Perl (1979) explored how writers write and concluded that composition is not straightforward and linear. Writing, they argued, should be a search for meaning, one that becomes clear only when the writer engages in a process over time. Their research provided the foundation of what came to be known as "the writing process," consisting of six stages writers follow when composing: (1) prewriting, (2) drafting, (3) sharing and feedback, (4) revising, (5) editing, and (6) finishing or publishing.

Arthur Applebee (1986) sums up the 1970s as a time that produced a "groundswell of support for 'process approaches' to learning to write" (p. 95). Teachers responded favorably to the new research, since traditional methods were not producing many inspired writers; students rarely wrote more than one draft, added or deleted details, or reorganized text. However, teachers did not immediately change their practices. The reason, Applebee argued, was the lack of professional materials and staff development opportunities available to them.

The 1980s

With landmark works such as Donald Graves's (1983) *Writing: Teachers and Children at Work*, Donald Murray's (1985) *A Writer Teaches Writing*, and Lucy Calkins's (1986) *The Art of Teaching Writing*, the professional literature took a huge step in this decade toward showing teachers how to apply the writing process. Examples of effective instructional strategies filled these books, allowing teachers an inside view into some exceptional classrooms. These authors based their ideas on the notion that young writers must think for themselves—and must write for clear purposes in a variety of modes and formats.

They also advocated conferring with students and having them share with peers after drafting. Both teachers and researchers noticed improvement in writing when students received meaningful feedback on drafts and learned how to apply revision and editing skills to strengthen their writing (Graves, 1983). In short, the work of authors, researchers, and teachers proved that the writing process is not a rigid series of steps; rather, it's a menu of flexible, recursive actions writers take to make their message clear and memorable.

During the mid-1980s, the phrase *traits of writing* was coined to describe the qualities that good writing possesses: ideas, organization, voice, word choice, sentence fluency, conventions, and presentation. The traits grew out of observations of writing—what worked and what didn't—and the levels of proficiency that students at different ages and levels of skill demonstrated in their work. Finally, teachers had a language to describe what writing should be, so they could help students reach the standards for writing that were increasingly present in their teaching lives. (More about the traits and their effectiveness can be found in chapter 3, page 32.)

The 1990s

The 1990s brought a proliferation of professional books, such as Ralph Fletcher's (1992) *What a Writer Needs*, Donald Graves's (1994) *A Fresh Look at Writing*, and Lucy Calkins's (1994) new edition of *The Art of Teaching Writing*, which refined and extended ideas for teaching writing. The writing workshop, first described in Donald Graves's (1983) *Writing: Teachers and Children at Work* and depicted so vividly in Nancie Atwell's (1987) *In the Middle*, emerged as a favored structure for implementing a process approach to instruction. The workshop typically includes minilessons on writing craft; teacher modeling; student choice of topic, mode, and genre; extended time to draft, revise, and edit; and individual and small-group conferences. For better or worse, publishers jumped on the bandwagon and produced a plethora of curriculum materials inspired by the workshop model.

The 1990s was also the decade of standards, which were recommended and in some instances demanded at the national and state levels. Those standards grew out of English language arts (ELA) scope and sequence guidelines that varied across districts and states. Realizing the value of having common standards for teaching and learning, the International Reading Association and the National Council of Teachers of English (1996) took the bold and controversial step of creating a joint document, *Standards for the English Language Arts*, which provides national standards that embrace the writing process and recommends that "students employ a wide range of strategies as they write and use different writing process elements appropriately to communicate with different audiences for a variety of purposes" (p. 25).

The traits of writing grew in popularity in this decade as an accurate and reliable assessment model used by individual teachers and whole states, including Arizona, Washington, Kansas, and Oregon, to name a few. Other states, such as Texas, New York, South Carolina, and Illinois, adapted the model to meet their needs.

Even more significant was the discovery that when the traits are taught, not just assessed, student writing dramatically improves (Arter, Spandel, Culham, & Pollard, 1994).

2000 to Today

With the interest in writing riding high, it's not surprising that assessments of all sizes and shapes emerged to measure how well students were meeting the standards. As such, the millennial decade will undoubtedly be remembered as the testing decade. Some of those assessments provided an authentic glimpse of students' writing capabilities by allowing ample time for writing and choice of topics, but most provided little more than the dull rumble of collective data. Sadly, the gold standard of teaching writing using the writing process within a writing workshop was often cast aside in favor of teaching to the test, a practice that rarely produces the desired result: strong writers. In fact, experts agree that a razor-sharp focus on teaching writing based only on what is on the test provides students with a lightweight writing education and often leaves them behind, rather than moving them toward meeting critical writing standards.

The Traits

The traits—ideas, organization, voice, word choice, sentence fluency, conventions, and presentation—represented a huge breakthrough because, for the first time, writing teachers could link assessment with instruction in a purposeful, meaningful way. They are sometimes referred to as 6+1, because there are six core traits plus one (presentation) that is a small motor and visual skill; together, they represent the range of skills needed in strong pieces of writing.

Teaching students how to revise and edit their own work was finally in our grasp. The traits provided that critical missing link between the writing process and writing workshop, on one hand, and the language needed to help students understand how writing works and how it is produced, regardless of its purpose or form or the context in which it is produced, on the other. No wonder teachers have embraced the traits so widely from coast to coast—they work. They make sense. And they help students improve in ways that produce the results teachers and administrators crave. Today, the traits are present in one form or another in most state writing assessments, in the National Assessment of Educational Progress (NAEP), and in the writing component of the SAT and ACT.

This discovery parallels what research tells us: direct instruction in revision and editing strategies, supported by guided practice, is essential to helping students apply the writing process with success (Applebee, 1986; Atwell, 1987; Calkins, 1986; Cramer, 2001; DeFoe, 2000; Pritchard & Honeycutt, 2006). And "although most researchers agree that the strategies and mental processes involved in the writing process are recursive and interlocked," as Ruie J. Pritchard and Ronald L. Honeycutt (2006) note, "many have discovered that studying one component at a time makes an enormously complex task more manageable" (p. 281). Simply put, those components are the traits.

Although this bird's-eye view of the evolution of writing instruction and the traits of writing is greatly abridged, you can see the fascinating journey that teachers have been on, leading us to the era of Common Core State Standards and a renewed interest in, and passion for, the most effective methods of teaching writing.

Chapter Organization

This book is organized into chapters that explore what is happening in writing instruction today and how that impacts the classroom and school. We'll look at dynamic practices for writing and how to integrate them into your school's writing curriculum and practice. You'll sample assessments and get specific help in what to look for and what to say to teachers about writing instruction. You'll gather critical information and insights about why teaching writing is hard but not impossible.

Chapter 1 examines the research behind the impacts on today's writing classroom and the different forms and purposes of writing assessment. Chapter 2 details how the Common Core State Standards will change the teaching and learning of writing, including working with English learners and making critical reading and writing connections throughout the curriculum. Chapter 3 introduces best practices for writing instruction—the 4Ws of writing: writing process, writing workshop, writing traits, and writing modes. Chapters 4 and 5 explore the assessment of the writing of students, the writing program at the school, and teachers' readiness to deliver high-quality instruction. Chapter 6 provides tools to help you recognize the strengths and areas of need in your school's writing program. Finally, the book closes with a glossary of helpful writing terms. Throughout, you will find reproducible scoring guides and other resources (which you may also download at **go.solution-tree .com/leadership**).

ONE

ASSESSMENT AND THE WRITING CLASSROOM

Assessments. Test scores. They are fundamental to education in these times. Students know what is important by what is graded or what is on the test. Teachers, likewise, look to the assessments to know what they must teach. The Common Core State Standards and subsequent assessments send a strong message that writing is important and once again at the forefront of instruction across every content area. By using the traits for assessment and instruction, we help students build thinking and shape ideas into complex, highly individual, polished products. If formally assessing student writing is what it takes to return writing to its rightful place, bring it on!

—Carol Hailey McLean, K–12 Reading/Language Arts
Resource Specialist, Shawnee Mission School District,
Johnson County, Kansas

Writing instruction has come of age. For many years, reading instruction dominated the research literature on literacy. However, a growing number of books and reports document the importance of writing and the most effective ways to teach it. These include the following: *Because Writing Matters* from the National Writing Project and Carl Nagin (2003), *The Neglected "R"* from the National Commission on Writing (2003), *Writing Next* from the Alliance for Excellent Education (Graham & Perin, 2007), the summary report from the National Assessment of Educational Progress (National Center for Education Statistics, 2012), *Writing Now* from the NCTE (2008), the Common Core State Standards Initiative (National Governors Association Center for Best Practices [NGA] & Council of Chief State School Officers [CCSSO], 2010), and *Informing Writing* (Graham et al., 2011). The consensus is that, though we have made strides, we have a long way to go to create classrooms that meet the needs of today's students. Citing troubling statistics, these publications concur that many writing classes are failing students in key areas.

What We Must Do

We must change the way we teach and assess writing in schools. I completely agree with Steve Graham, Karen Harris, and Michael Hebert (2011) when they state, "Writing is not just an option for young people; it is essential" (p. 10). The recommendations discussed in the following sections stem from critical research findings in support of writing instruction reform.

Give Complex, Relevant Writing Tasks Requiring Analysis and Synthesis

Findings confirm that a steady stream of worksheets and prompts still dominate the teaching of writing, despite the fact that we know using them does not lead to thoughtful, complex prose. Instead, these methods reinforce the notion that writing is a simple task whose purpose is to satisfy the teacher (Graham & Perin, 2007; National Commission on Writing, 2003). Sadly, this is not new information. In the 1980s, educational researcher George Hillocks Jr. (1986) concluded that "exercises in declarative knowledge likely had negative effects on writing quality because, in many instances, they supplanted opportunities for students to actually engage in writing" (p. 225).

If students are to learn to think, reason, and communicate, they should be encouraged to use writing as a means to discover what matters. They must "struggle with details, wrestle with the facts, and rework raw information and dimly understood concepts" (National Commission on Writing, 2003, p. 9). This does not happen through repetitive skill-and-drill exercises and endless prompts. It happens when teachers understand that writing is thinking on paper and provide rich and diverse opportunities for students to practice that thinking.

Help Students Perform Beyond a Basic Level

The NAEP writing assessment puts students on a continuum of writing levels from "below basic" to "basic" to "proficient" to "advanced." The report reveals that only 27 percent of eighth graders are proficient writers (National Center for Education Statistics, 2012). Furthermore, it points out that only three writers in a hundred achieved the distinction of advanced. And to compound matters, in the results reported for grade 12, those numbers did not improve—not even by one percentage point.

Why are students struggling with writing? Even on the NAEP assessment, where students are allowed access to technology and write for different purposes and audiences, an alarmingly low number demonstrate writing proficiency. This may be because our expectations are too low, and we've been bamboozled into thinking that preparing students for state writing tests is all that is necessary. It clearly isn't—not by a long shot. Or it might be that we are failing to provide essential instructional elements that foster the complex thinking and learning required for excellence in writing. The NAEP (National Center for Education Statistics, 2012),

Writing Next (Graham & Perin, 2007), and *The Neglected "R"* (National Commission on Writing, 2003) reports cite both of these reasons, among others, for the disappointing performance of students in grades 8 and 12.

In part to ensure that today's student writers outperform their peers in past decades, the Common Core State Standards lay out a rigorous set of benchmarks designed to create diverse and purpose-driven tasks built on a foundation of writing process and complex thinking skills. A vast majority of states—including some that have not shored up their expectations of student writing—have embraced the CCSS. Curriculum alignment with the CCSS, or their equivalent, is occurring across the United States. Standards are on the rise, and writing instruction is in focus. Professional educators at every level are asking, "How do we improve student writing performance to meet more rigorous standards?"

Ensure That Students Have Enough Time for Writing

Arthur Applebee, Judith Langer, Martin Nystrand, and Adam Gamoran (2003) report that we are not providing students with the time they need to become skilled writers, stating that two-thirds of students spend less than an hour each week writing in or out of school. Jennifer Gilbert and Steve Graham (2010) note that a survey of fourth-, fifth-, and sixth-grade teachers found that only about fifteen minutes per day were spent explicitly teaching writing. In *Writing Next*, Steven Graham and Delores Perin (2007) point out that the total time students spend writing is equal to only about 15 percent of the time they spend watching television. How, then, are students to become effective writers who can analyze and synthesize information? Spending more time teaching students how to write, giving them time to write for different purposes, and providing targeted feedback are essential if students are to improve.

As part of its national writing agenda, *The Neglected "R"* report recommends that we "double the amount of time most students spend writing and require successful completion of a course in writing theory and practice as a condition of teacher licensing" (National Commission on Writing, 2003, p. 3). These are certainly worthy goals: more time for students to write *and* for teachers to learn how to teach writing.

Apply Technology to the Teaching of Writing

As I travel the United States visiting schools, I see evidence of a technological revolution. Document cameras, laptop computers, iPads, and LCD projectors are coming in the front door, while chalkboards, overhead projectors, and plain old whiteboards are going out the back. Classrooms are even moving aside electronic whiteboards, formerly the darling of classroom digital technology, for more reliable, more adaptable, and more affordable options. The consistent claim of the National Commission on Writing (2003) is that "national technological infrastructure for education is as critical to the United States in the twenty-first century as highways were in the twentieth" (p. 4). Teachers are excited about these innovations, but in the quiet of late afternoon, they often confide that's it's all going so fast it's hard to keep up. One thing we are certain of, however, is that the digital assessments that accompany the Common Core State Standards will usher in a whole new need for assessment literacy.

Students, on the other hand, seek every opportunity to use technology, figuring it out as they go. In *From Digital Natives to Digital Wisdom*, Marc Prensky (2012) explains that because today's students are immersed in technology, they have developed cognitive thinking patterns that differ from ours and are therefore less intimidated by new electronic devices. Interestingly, however, they don't regard much of what they create with those devices, such as emails, text messages, and instant messages, as writing. This disconnect is significant, because students themselves believe that good writing is an essential skill and that more writing instruction would be helpful to them (Lenhart, Arafeh, Smith, & Macgill, 2008). If students believe that writing matters in the real world but don't view electronic communications as writing, we must broaden their definition. This generation's affinity for technology defines them as learners, and tapping into that affinity is critical to teaching them to write.

Show Teachers How to Change Practice

In *Because Writing Matters*, members of the National Writing Project and Carl Nagin (2003) synthesize writing research and describe its implications for teachers and administrators. A persistent theme throughout this document is the urgent need for high-quality training, supported by evidence that few preservice and practicing teachers of English and content areas receive more than a token amount of training in writing instruction. Yet teachers are expected to teach writing and to use what students create as a means to assess what they know and can do. *Writing Now*, the policy research brief of the NCTE (2008), advises that schools should examine current practices and reform them. Teaching writing skills such as grammar in isolation (outside the context of meaningful writing for significant purposes and real audiences), for example, should be discarded in favor of teaching writing as a holistic process using a context-based functional approach. The NCTE policy research brief further advises that the process model of writing should be flexible and include a metacognitive component in which students reflect on their own writing performances rather than follow the static, linear model from prewriting to drafting and revising that is present in many classrooms today.

Writing may well be how we connect the dots in learning, but unless students have teachers who know how to nurture and support them, and writing teachers have administrators who know how to help them succeed, it is difficult to envision a future that is much different from the present.

Administer Fair and Meaningful Assessments

To be effective writing teachers, it is critical that we understand what students can and can't do. To accomplish this, we need a highly reliable and accurate assessment tool. Enter the traits of writing. After being applied and refined for more than twenty-five years, the trait model is now the gold standard of classroom-based analytic writing assessment. (To give you a sense of how this process works, sample papers from primary, upper elementary, and middle school are assessed on pages 38–42.)

As large-scale state assessments that aim to pinpoint achievement in math, reading, writing, and other key subject areas have rolled into our schools—and *over* many teachers—they've stolen precious time for instruction. Teachers need better formative assessment tools—ones that will help them plan and execute instruction. As an administrator, you can help them understand that when they teach writing well, it will show up on the state test or the national assessment. It will. You know it, I know it, and teachers need to know—and believe—it with all their hearts.

Large-scale assessments have their place; they inform us in broad strokes how specific writing skills are progressing. But make no mistake—formative classroom assessment drives instruction. We need both, and we need to understand the role of teachers as we seek to move forward in writing instruction.

Regardless of the grade, skill, or experience of the teacher, the following core principles are keys to the success of any writing program:

- **We must speak a common language based on the traits**—Respond to student writing according to individual traits, using the same language from day to day and year to year to develop a deep understanding of how writing works

- **We must nurture process learning**—Value process over product in the classroom, and encourage and celebrate writing every day

- **We must use criteria to set the standard**—Use criteria or clear indicators to describe what we believe students must learn and to measure their progress

The Role of Large-Scale Assessments

Exciting conversations about writing instruction are happening in teachers' rooms across the United States. As the CCSS (NGA & CCSSO, 2010) rolled out for writing, new energy to reform writing instruction was infused into these discussions. But when the topic turns from classroom practice to large-scale, high-stakes assessments, the conversation often comes to a grinding halt. Everyone—students, teachers, administrators, parents, and community members—is impacted by large-scale assessments. Although their form varies from state to state, and now with the anticipated entrance of the assessment component of the Common Core, their purpose is the same: to determine how well students are meeting clearly defined and enumerated standards for writing. It's a huge national effort that costs untold millions of dollars each year.

We can only hope that the CCSS assessments on the horizon will reflect best practices in assessment and serve to strengthen writing programs and the way writing is taught. Surely, the days when students are told to do a timed writing based on a prompt that they care little about are gone. In its place will be a complex task that draws upon reading and writing and that integrates complex thinking skills. One thing is for sure: the assessments are coming, and they will be expensive. If we've learned nothing else from the assessment mania in our schools, it is that the assessments will follow the standards and will drain precious resources of time and money. We can only hope that this next generation of assessments is richly useful to every stakeholder: students, parents, teachers, administrators, and the community at large.

Researchers and authors P. David Pearson, Devon Brenner, and Linda Rief explain that "standardized tests probably do serve the needs of the general public and policy makers when they try to answer the question, How are our schools doing?" (Brenner, Pearson, & Rief, 2007, p. 261). Taxpayers rightly demand to know their investment is paying off, that students are meeting and perhaps even exceeding the standards. Assessment provides accountability, plain and simple.

Now for the bad news: since large-scale, high-stakes assessments have such a high public profile, they often become the de facto curriculum in many classrooms. "Teachers defer to the test designers as the experts, and embrace the test itself as the curriculum," notes researcher George Hillocks Jr. (2002, p. 198). These teachers address only those skills necessary to pass the test. They administer practice tests over and over, hoping this repetition will improve student scores. And it doesn't. In fact, according to Tommy Thomason and Carol York (2000), students often do worse, because they fall victim to testing fatigue.

We can't surrender the curriculum to test makers; it's far too important. So let me emphasize: the test is not a curriculum, and neither are the CCSS. In fact, in the Common Core State Standards' own words, "The Standards define what all students should know and do, not how teachers should teach" (NGA & CCSSO, 2010, p. 7). The standards should guide writing instruction, serving teachers and students as they work together in the writing process classroom toward shared goals. The assessment component of the CCSS should serve students and teachers and support learning using best practices; it should not become a means to an end: high test scores. As Kylene Beers, Robert Probst, and Linda Rief note (2007), a mismatch exists between what assessments could potentially do (celebrate accomplishments) and what they do all too often (highlight failures).

We want and need good writers, not just good test takers. "When rubrics are used only to assign students numbers," Chris Gallagher and Amy Lee (2008) remind us, "they are counterproductive" (p. 159). I would take their wise point a step further: when assessment becomes the de facto curriculum, we have lost our way.

Holistic Versus Analytic Scoring

Large-scale assessments were often scored holistically. That means trained scorers ranked and sorted student writing, using a single rubric or scoring guide, to provide a simple answer to complex questions such as "Are students meeting the standards?" and "Are groups of students improving overall?" Note I am using past tense in this paragraph. I can almost guarantee that the assessments for CCSS will not be holistic. They will be analytic assessments based on criteria that mirror the complex tasks in reading and writing students will be asked to complete.

However, holistic assessment scoring can be used in today's schools for the following purposes:

- **To gain insight about an entire group's performance**—"Our eighth graders have improved overall" or "The fourth grade outperformed the third."

- **To show how many students have met or exceeded the standards at different grade levels**—"Twelve percent of the eighth-grade class did not meet the writing standard; 59 percent met the standard; 29 percent exceeded the standard."

- **To rank and sort individual performances**—"Jayson received the highest score, while Mita got the lowest."

- **To place students into district- and school-level programs like talented and gifted, advanced placement, special needs, and Title I**—"Jesus shows exceptional writing skills and should be considered for advanced placement in language arts."

- **To grade using percentages, points, or letters such as A, B, C, D, and F**—"Latonya is now working in the 'B' range, with an 83 percentage average in writing."

Holistic scores are valid and useful but broad. They do not provide specific diagnostic information to guide instruction.

Analytic assessment is individualized, focused, and precise because it requires us to look at writing from multiple perspectives. Like scorers of holistic assessments, scorers of analytic assessments use a rubric or scoring guide. But they use those rubrics and scoring guides to determine multiple scores for a piece of writing, rather than just one. The trait model is a form of analytic assessment. In my thirty-five years of teaching and researching, the traits—ideas, organization, voice, word choice, sentence fluency, conventions, and presentation—are the best analytic model I've found.

Analytic scoring is used to provide formative assessment information:

- **To provide details about individual students' writing performance and to document progress over time**—"Lily, the amount of progress you've made this year in organization and word choice is remarkable!"

- **To target strengths and weaknesses that inform instruction**—"Frankie has learned to narrow his idea but needs to add detail" or "Le has mastered punctuation but is struggling with spelling."

- **To give the writer specific, focused feedback that will help him or her revise and edit**—"What if you moved this part to the very beginning to create a stronger lead, Raheem? Try it, and see if that organization choice improves the piece."

- **To confer with students about their writing progress**—"Sara, look at how much more you know now about word choice and using use words well than you did at the beginning of the year!"

- **To develop classroom lessons designed to teach and reinforce specific skills**— "Harper, would you read your terrific first paragraph to the class, so people can hear the different ways you began each sentence? That's something we all need to work on."

It is yet to be determined what form the assessment component of the CCSS will take, but it is safe to assume that, like the standards themselves, it will emphasize complexity and rigor. From early indications, the assessments will likely be analytic in form, producing results that respect the complexity of writing well. Samples of the CCSS assessments suggest that they will be much like a driver's test. A driver's test consists of knowledge about driving (the written exam) and the ability to drive (the road test). All indications are that students will need to know a lot of information about writing but will also need to be able to take it on the road—to produce high-quality text in a variety of modes, genres, and formats.

In the next chapter, I'll dive into what we know about the CCSS in writing and how this national initiative impacts writing instruction practices. We'll take a look at the writing standards and their connection to reading through the eyes of teaching and learning for all students, including English learners and students with special needs.

TWO

WRITING IN THE COMMON CORE ERA

Teachers at schools where writing is taught successfully collaborate. They vertically score writing samples based on agreed-upon rubrics, participate in conversations based upon student writing, and plan purposefully for instruction. Assessment is a pivotal part of every teacher's day and informs every decision teachers make, as they work together to meet the Common Core State Standards, about what happens next for student writers. Writing is embedded in daily lesson plans and curriculum maps. When curriculum maps are revised to include Common Core standards, planning for writing is explicit.

—Valerie Truesdale, Superintendent, Beaufort County
School District, and Jamie Pinckney, Principal, Okatie
Elementary School, Beaufort, South Carolina

By summer 2013, forty-five states had adopted the Common Core State Standards, three short years after their publication, making them a national initiative and platform for educational reform unlike any other. Besides the standards' obvious influence in how teaching and learning decisions will be shaped from this time forward, it is interesting to note the powerful role they give to writing not only as a subject of its own, but within other subjects as a way to show what is learned. No longer relegated to the folding card table with the other content areas at the family dinner, writing now takes its rightful place with the grown-ups: reading and math. There is a renewed energy for teaching writing and improving student writing skills across the United States—even in states that did not adopt the Common Core.

For every grade, the CCSS provide standards within these four domains:

1. **Text Types and Purposes**—Narrative, informational/explanatory, and argument in diverse print and electronic formats. (In Common Core terms, these are narrative, informational, and opinion/argument, respectively.)

2. **Production and Distribution of Writing**—The writing process (prewriting, drafting, sharing and feedback, revising, editing, and finishing or publishing) and traits (ideas, organization, voice, word choice, sentence fluency, conventions, and presentation)

3. **Research to Build and Present Knowledge**—Writing in all modes and across the content areas that requires acquisition of information from print and electronic resources, synthesis, and written interpretation of what was learned

4. **Range of Writing**—Short, midrange, and long-term assignments and projects for many different purposes in a variety of formats

As schools grapple with implementing these domains and each grade level's standards, they must examine current practice, keeping what is effective and discarding the rest in favor of teaching that produces the kind of thoughtful, complex texts that nearly all students are capable of producing. Now that we have a new set of standards, school writing instruction must regroup and figure out the best way to meet and exceed those standards in every classroom and subject area.

Content Area Writing

The Common Core State Standards go even further than these four targets. They make it clear that writing in the content areas is a critical literacy skill, making it more urgent than ever to teach all teachers how to effectively teach and use writing strategies in their classrooms. Both science and social studies standards within the CCSS reference the ELA standards, making it more urgent than ever to teach content teachers key writing strategies. In reports such as *Writing to Read* (Graham & Hebert, 2010), we learn that writing about material read or presented in science, social studies, and other content classes enhances comprehension and learning. Writing is therefore a critical method for achieving goals and learning targets in content classes.

This notion of writing in the content areas has been around for a long time. Attention to it grew in the 1980s and in the millennium decade. Two notable movements (which didn't gain much traction) are Writing Across the Curriculum and Writing in the Content Areas. These efforts fell short in clarifying that science and social studies teachers didn't need to become mini-English teachers. In all fairness, there is a reason they didn't become English teachers in the first place. Their interests lie with their content—be it science, social studies, health or physical education, the arts, or whatever area has been their focus of study. The administrator's job is simply to convince the science teacher that when students write for purposes that satisfy the science curriculum, the learning experience is enriched. The point is, and always should have been, that students will be better served meeting the standards of any given content area by writing.

Like reading, writing is the job of every teacher. And as with reading, it's critical that all teachers have access to the tools and knowledge to teach students how to write about content.

The CCSS have spoken. This is how schools are supposed to approach content writing. From a more realistic perspective, however, teachers will need support and encouragement, along with the sophisticated skill of knowing how and when to use writing in their various disciplines. No one should expect them to become first-class writing instructors overnight; your job as the administrator is to know how to help teachers achieve the shared goal—students who write well no matter the subject. Content writing is a huge area of development for schools and worthy of a text of its own. However, as you approach this work, take heart. In this critical area, my experience with the traits of writing persuades me that the ideas in this book will work for content teachers just as well as they will work for you.

English Learners and Students With Special Needs

The CCSS do not try to define the range of activities and lessons that best support learners new to English. Nor do they establish the scope of what writing instruction should cover for students with special needs. Rather, the standards recognize that teachers must have a rich array of teaching strategies to meet the needs of *every* learner; they must create a classroom that respects the pace at which all students learn—from the one who struggles most to the one who sails off the top of the chart. The standards do not exempt English learners from high-quality writing goals:

> The National Governors Association Center for Best Practices and the Council of Chief State Officers strongly believe that all students should be held to the same high expectations of the Common Core State Standards. This includes students who are English language learners. However, these students may require additional time, appropriate instructional support and aligned assessments as they acquire both English language proficiency and content area knowledge. (NGA & CCSSO, n.d.a)

A similar statement addresses students with special needs: "Students with disabilities—students eligible under the Individuals with Disabilities Act (IDEA)—must be challenged to excel within the general curriculum and be prepared for success in their post-school lives, including college and/or careers" (Center for the Education and Study of Diverse Populations [CESDP], 2013). The NGA and CCSSO's (n.d.a) statement goes on to explain that "the continued development of understanding about research-based instructional practices and a focus on their effective implementation will help improve access to mathematics and English language arts (ELA) standards for all students, including those with disabilities."

Although English learners and students with special needs may not learn how to write at the same rate or through traditional methods of instruction, they can and will show great gains from instruction based on formative assessment and through the focused lessons and activities outlined on pages 36–43 that are based on dynamic practices.

Understanding how writing develops, from the first early markings on a page to detailed and elaborated works, is a key to helping those who struggle for whatever reason. The continuum of writing development captured in the Teacher-Friendly Scoring Guide for Beginning Writers (pages 44–50) provides insight into what these youngest students know and what they are ready to learn at any given stage of their development. Regardless of students' ages, these scoring guides can be a useful jumping-off place for teachers of students with limited English language skills. Whether you are five or fifteen, a sequence of skills defines what typical writers do as they are first learning to write Standard English. This is where teachers should anchor students who are, for whatever reason, at the beginning of their writing lives.

It is my belief, formed from firsthand experience and research, that English learners and students with special needs benefit from the best teaching about writing, which includes the following:

- Modeling, modeling, modeling

- Talking and oral communication

- Mentor texts

- Small-group work

- One-on-one time with the teacher and other students

- Word banks, word walls, word lists, and other places to gather words and phrases for use in writing

- Scaled-down assignments that allow students to develop skills in writing but don't overwhelm

- Specific targets to work on that allow students to focus on individual writing skills that accumulate over time

- High standards and expectations

- Time to develop and grow as a writer

- Evidence of growth, no matter where the writer begins

- Positive, supportive writing environment

In other words, students with special needs grow the fastest with the best teaching. The needs of these fragile and often reluctant writers are not all that different from the other writers in the classroom. They need a wide berth to experiment and try different methods of writing, without high stakes hanging over their heads. They need to develop a big bag of writing techniques and skills. They need to understand how writing works and what it should look like as they write for a variety of different purposes and audiences. They need the traits even more than the average writer, in fact, because the traits give them a language to find their way into the writing world—a world that may at first feel unfriendly and unsafe for them as learners with specific challenges.

There is no silver bullet for working with writers who are behind for whatever reason. But noting progress and making nudges that move students forward make a big difference in meeting goals and standards. Teachers must let students know how their efforts to learn English are progressing and what to do next. Students' efforts in writing must be valued and respected regardless of their level of performance. That is a fundamental role that you can play as the administrator. Knowing how to talk about writing, recognize signs of success, and establish the importance of writing in students' lives comes from the top and filters down to every teacher and learner.

A word or two about technology in reference to the learning needs of English learners or students with special needs: it helps. Laptops, desktops, iPads, tablets, smartphones, digital cameras, interactive whiteboards, and whatever else is around the corner—these all make a huge difference in terms of engaging and encouraging writers, no matter their level of proficiency.

The research into technology and learning is crystal clear: from the first studies of word processing in the 1980s to the wealth of information currently available about how to infuse digital learning into teaching, there is consensus that the constructive use of technology supports writers at every age and level of ability. What further evidence do we need than the fact that for both reading and writing the CCSS assessments will be delivered through electronic media? Technology is here, it's powerful, and it's a huge motivator for learning.

The Reading and Writing Connection

The CCSS build an easy-to-navigate bridge between reading and writing; important intersections in the standards connect these two vital processes. Researcher Pilar Duran Escribano (1999) explains that "reading puts the learner in touch with other minds so that he can experience the ways in which writers have organized information, selected words and structured arguments" (p. 62). Donald Hall and Donald Emblen (1994), renowned poets, writers, and writing teachers, say it this way: "Reading well precedes writing well" (p. xxi). Along with scores of other respected researchers and practitioners in the field, these writers draw the same conclusion: read, read, read, so you can write, write, write.

Writers must marinate in carefully honed words to explore their own ideas and the best ways to express them. They learn the language by hearing it done beautifully. They understand the power that the right word in the right place can bring to the reader's understanding. Drawing from models we call mentor texts—texts that can teach the reader something about writing—they find new ways to make their own ideas come to life. Yes, writers learn through the carefully constructed lessons their teachers provide, but most of all, they learn how writing works by reading and examining texts.

This is especially important for students whose second language is English. For these children and young adults, the sound and flow of English is not natural, as it is to native speakers and writers. For a long time, as they work to perfect Standard English skills, they hear their primary language in their heads, so as they write—even when they have acquired enough words to express ideas—their fluency may be halting and stilted. Reading aloud a lot and experiencing many oral language opportunities build understanding of how the language works, both in form and content. Such experiences make it easier for English learners to replicate Standard English in their own writing.

Reading and writing are inextricably linked. According to a study carried out by Sy-ying Lee and Stephen Krashen (2004) titled "Competence in Foreign Language Writing," a person's reading level can predict his or her writing skills. "Reading provides writers with knowledge of the language of writing, the grammar, vocabulary, and discourse style writers use," they purport. They further advise, "[This] conclusion is consistent with a number of studies in both first language and second language development showing that those who read more acquire more of the written language" (p. 10).

Conversely, we know that writing improves reading. According to research reported by Steve Graham and Michael Hebert in *Writing to Read*, from the 2010 report by the Carnegie Foundation, "increasing how much students write does in fact improve how well they read" (p. 20). We know, of course, the first reader of a text is the writer him- or herself. These two critical literacy processes support each other hand-in-glove, which is good news in today's schools, where time is critical and resources scant. A classroom library built to support the different ability levels of readers can, in turn, support writers as they move from beginning stages of writing to more advanced methods of expressing themselves for a variety of purposes.

Administrators who wisely support teachers' efforts to build print and nonprint reading resources in the classroom can feel confident that there are writing gains to be made from those same materials. Teachers will need support and suggestions for how to make those connections clear to students, but the reasons for exploring the link between reading and writing are like low-hanging fruit. Pick them. There is great bounty waiting to be harvested.

In chapter 3, we'll explore dynamic practices in writing instruction, or what I like to call the 4Ws: writing process, writing workshop, writing traits, and writing modes. Learning how to artfully weave these dynamic practices together into one cohesive whole is the holy grail for writing teachers. By understanding a little about each of the 4Ws, you will discover ways to support and encourage teachers to succeed on this quest.

THREE

DYNAMIC WRITING INSTRUCTION

When teachers are able to refine their own craft through the use of trait-based instruction, they are able to engage students in lessons and inspire them to create rich and authentic texts. The traits help students view themselves as writers, which is a powerful association that sustains interest and energy during the writing process. This collaborative process between teachers and students is what unites them as a community of writers.

—Erin Bailey, Instructional Coach, Blue Springs School District, Missouri

Understanding the 4Ws—writing process, writing workshop, writing traits, and writing modes—is the key to understanding what to look for and promote in dynamic writing instruction. These terms and the kind of teaching and learning that they represent are the key to a high-quality writing program in your schools. Here are some quick definitions.

1. **Writing process:** A series of recursive steps that writers go through to generate text. Generally, we know them as prewriting, drafting, sharing and feedback, revising, editing, and finishing or publishing.

2. **Writing workshop:** A flexible structure for organizing time in the writing classroom. The writing workshop includes whole-group instruction on writing craft (key qualities of the trait) and extended opportunities for students to write on individual pieces, with time for conferring with the teacher.

3. **Writing traits:** The common language for the writing classroom and the criteria by which writing is assessed. The seven traits are (1) ideas, (2) organization, (3) voice, (4) word choice, (5) sentence fluency, (6) conventions, and (7) presentation.

Each is broken down into four key qualities (pages 25–26), which are the focus of assessment and instruction.

4. **Writing modes:** The purposes for writing—narrative, informational/explanatory, or argument. The mode is the overarching reason why writers write specific texts and describes what they plan to accomplish. According to George Hillocks Jr. (2002), these modes help the writer make that purpose clear to the reader. Go to pages 24–25 for a closer look at each of the modes.

Integrating the 4Ws

Although there is general agreement that the 4Ws are at the core of a successful writing classroom, it's rare to see all four integrated and operating smoothly. Teachers often grab onto a writing workshop model, for instance, without really thinking about what the content or focus or minilessons should be. Others migrate toward a traits approach but don't understand that the writing process is the driving force underneath their trait-specific assessment and instruction.

They don't understand, for example, that when we use the traits, we are able to construct an approach to assessing and teaching writing that works within the writing process, making that ever-elusive step of revision more transparent for teaching and learning. Table 3.1 shows how these two Ws work together.

Table 3.1: Relationship of the Writing Process to the Writing Traits

Writing Process	Predominant Writing Traits
Prewriting: The writer comes up with a topic and determines the mode (narrative, informational/explanatory, or argument).	Ideas, organization, and voice
Drafting: The writer commits his or her ideas to paper in rough form.	Word choice and sentence fluency
Sharing and feedback: The writer gets feedback on the draft from the reader or listener.	Ideas, organization, voice, word choice, and sentence fluency
Revising: The writer reflects on the draft and makes choices that lead to a clearer, more engaging piece.	Ideas, organization, voice, word choice, and sentence fluency
Editing: The writer cleans up the piece, checking for correct spelling, capitalization, punctuation, paragraphing, and grammar and usage.	Conventions
Finishing or publishing: The writer creates a final copy and takes it public.	Presentation

To become better writers, students need to understand all these steps, particularly the difference between revision and editing. They should learn about writing and apply what they know in the writing workshop format, where teachers and students work to develop extended pieces of writing over time. Those workshop pieces should be purpose-driven—that is, they should show strength in the narrative, informational/explanatory, or argument modes. We weave it all together so it's doable, manageable, and most of all, gets the writing results we want and need.

It's taken four decades for me to understand how the writing traits, the writing process, and writing workshop originated and are interrelated and how the modes of writing—the purposes—fit into that equation. Let me try to outline what it might look like to teach writing by embracing each *W* in a classroom or across a school.

A System of Teaching

To help students become better writers, teachers need to understand the steps in the writing process, and they need instruction on the key qualities of the traits—along with opportunities to apply them in their own work. They need to work in a writing process classroom, preferably one organized in a writing workshop format. To support these efforts, there are prepackaged, ready-to-go writing materials galore out there, but before you spend your money, remember that "stuff" doesn't improve writing. *Writing* improves writing. Decades of research and classroom observation prove it (Graves, 1994).

Teaching students to write by writing takes time. You need a system like the one outlined in table 3.2 that is built on dynamic practices but is manageable and gets the results you want. It should also be a system that serves all students—those who excel at writing and those who don't—and blends process with traits, so that students learn how to think and talk about what they produce and revise and edit it accordingly.

Table 3.2: What Works and Doesn't Work in Teaching Writing

How Students Learn to Write	How Students Do Not Learn to Write
By watching the teacher model his or her own writing process	By being assigned writing with no attention to process
By practicing in the context of their own writing	By filling out worksheets and responding to isolated skill-and-drill practice
By writing to figure out what they know or want to know	By writing only to complete assignments
By using technology	By using only paper and pencil
By working, talking, and sharing with others	By working alone, silently
By focusing on process, the traits, and the modes	By focusing exclusively on product
By writing for real purposes and audiences, on topics that matter to them	By writing for purposes and audiences that are unclear, on topics they don't care about
By embracing revision and editing	By avoiding revision and editing and just turning it in
By understanding how to research and discover information that informs thinking and then relaying it in writing using their own words	By finding a source and copying it

A Daily Instructional Model

To implement a system that accomplishes dynamic practices in writing instruction, teachers must target specific skills that experienced writers use as they draft, revise, and edit. And they must make this process transparent for students, showing them how to use the key qualities of the traits to guide their thinking as they write.

Figure 3.1 shows a daily instructional model involving focus lessons, guided writing, and independent writing. These activities are explored in the following sections.

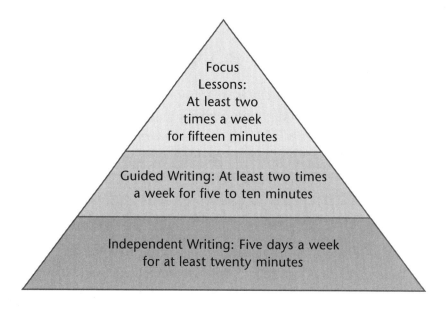

Figure 3.1: Daily instructional model.

Focus Lessons

A focus lesson is a short, teacher-led demonstration of a trait-specific or mode-related writing skill for the whole group. For a focus lesson, the teacher might break down the three Common Core text types—narrative, informational/explanatory, and argument—into greater detail.

- The narrative writer typically:
    - Offers a clear, well-developed story line
    - Includes characters that grow and change over time
    - Conveys time and setting effectively
    - Presents a conflict and resolution
    - Surprises, challenges, or entertains the reader
- The informational/explanatory writer typically:
    - Informs the reader about the topic
    - Transcends the obvious by explaining something interesting or curious about the topic
    - Focuses on making the topic clear for the reader
    - Anticipates and answers the reader's questions

  - Includes details that add information, support key ideas, and help the reader make personal connections

- The argument writer typically:

  - States a position clearly and sticks with it

  - Offers good, sound reasoning

  - Provides solid facts, opinions, and examples

  - Reveals weaknesses in other positions

  - Uses voice to add credibility and show confidence

In a mode-related focus lesson, the teacher might provide students with techniques and examples of how to go from a broad, general topic to one with a specific purpose. For example, a broad topic such as pets could become an opinion piece like "Why Dogs Make Better Pets Than Cats," an informational piece on the difference between wild and domesticated dogs, or a narrative with a dog for a main character. During these lessons, teachers help students to zero in on what they are writing: narrative, informational/explanatory, or argument.

Focus lessons also teach students how to write. This is where the traits and their key qualities are so useful. Students are taught specific moves writers make to improve their work for each trait. For example, the student who is writing the opinion piece on why dogs are better pets than cats learns how to work with ideas, organization, voice, word choice, sentence fluency, conventions, and presentation to develop a solid piece of writing. The key qualities of each trait break down the specific skills students need to learn to write a solid piece regardless of the purpose.

Following are the key qualities of the seven writing traits:

1. **Ideas**—The piece's content; its central message and details that support that message

   - Finding a topic

   - Focusing the topic

   - Developing the topic

   - Using details

2. **Organization**—The internal structure of the piece; the thread of logic: the pattern of meaning

   - Creating the lead

   - Using sequence words and transition words

   - Structuring the body

   - Ending with a sense of resolution

3. **Voice**—The tone and tenor of the piece; the personal stamp of the writer, which is achieved through a strong understanding of purpose and audience

   - Establishing a tone

   - Conveying the purpose

   - Creating a connection to the audience

   - Taking risks to create voice

4. **Word choice**—The vocabulary the writer uses to convey meaning and enlighten the reader

   - Applying strong verbs

   - Selecting striking words and phrases

   - Using specific and accurate words

   - Choosing words that deepen meaning

5. **Sentence fluency**—The structure of the sentences and the way words and phrases flow through the piece

   - Crafting well-built sentences

   - Varying sentence types

   - Capturing smooth and rhythmic flow

   - Breaking the rules to create fluency

6. **Conventions**—The mechanical correctness of the piece, including spelling, capitalization, punctuation, paragraphing, and grammar and usage

   - Checking spelling

   - Punctuating effectively and paragraphing accurately

   - Capitalizing correctly

   - Applying grammar and usage

7. **Presentation**—The physical appearance of the piece

   - Applying handwriting skills

   - Using word processing effectively

   - Making good use of white space

   - Refining text features

The best way to choose topics for focus lessons is by assessing student writing to figure out its strengths and weaknesses using the scoring guides in this book (pages 44–81 and online at **go.solution-tree.com/leadership**). That formative assessment will reveal what is working well and what still needs work. See pages 35–36 for an explanation of how to use the scoring guides.

Once teachers have assessed student work, they determine what lessons need to be taught and to whom. It might turn out, for example, that the assessment reveals only a handful of students struggle with crafting well-built sentences, a key quality of the sentence fluency trait. In that case, the teacher should prepare a focus lesson on this topic for a small group. Other key qualities may require whole-group instruction. This is the point of formative assessment: it shows teachers what students know and what they still need to learn.

Every student writer needs new and helpful instruction on the key qualities of the traits every year. It's possible to spiral instruction in the key qualities throughout the year, ensuring consistency across teachers and grades so students deepen their understanding of writing, rather than start over every year. Focus lessons are not a new idea, but organizing instruction systematically around them, trait by trait, just might be.

Guided Writing

The second component of the daily instructional model is guided writing. This is a critical step that provides much-needed scaffolding for students between focused instruction and independence using a new skill or a more complex application of the skill. Imagine watching a teacher present a focus lesson on a particular writing-related skill, such as using sequence and transition words effectively (a key quality for organization). The students are attentive. They listen as the teacher explains what sequence and transition words are and how to use them. They follow along as the teacher uses them in a draft of his or her own work and joins in on a lively discussion about what they notice. Then, to reinforce the skill, the teacher hands out a worksheet. Most students complete it successfully; however, when they write independently just a few minutes later, they don't apply the skill. What happened? It seemed like the lesson went so well!

Or did it? The intent of the lesson was for students to learn something about writing to use in their work, not to learn a skill and then ignore it. If the lesson was strong, and students understood what was being taught, why doesn't that new information about writing show up in their independent pieces? It's a source of great frustration for teachers, trust me. As it turns out, the secret to teaching and learning a new writing skill is to provide practice in the context of authentic writing. Yes! There is an answer: guided writing that takes place after instruction and before independent writing.

Judith Langer and Arthur Applebee (1986; Applebee, 2003), building on the work of Jerome Bruner (Wood, Bruner, & Ross, 1979) and Courtney Cazden (1979), use the metaphor of "instructional scaffolding" to describe this practice, in which students are presented with a task they can't do independently but could with the support of a skilled teacher. The teacher's goal is to wean students so they can carry out the task independently and try out new skills on drafts of their own writing—a step that is so essential to understanding and internalizing how writing works. Students need to practice skills, under the teacher's guidance, if they are expected to apply those skills to longer, more complex, self-generated projects.

Instead of worksheets, consider the value of guided writing using a dedicated writing folder. This is the ideal tool to help students gain new skills. In the folder, they store rough drafts to use for practicing revision and editing skills as they are taught. Teachers can implement this elegantly simple practice with little to no cost and without a lot of management.

The writing folder should contain two to four pieces of a student's own work in draft form. The papers should be rough, less than a page, and should come from quickwrites, literature responses, short-answer essays, and journal entries, among other sources. They can be pieces from any subject area; the key is that they are the student's own writing.

Think of the immediate benefit of a writing folder: If a student struggles and he or she is able to write only a sentence or two, then that is what is in the folder for practice. If the student is a skilled writer and generating longer, more complex text, then that is the writing on which he or she practices new skills. Because it is the student's own work, the folder automatically differentiates for levels of writing skill. Brilliant, right? The writing folder solves a myriad of teaching problems, affording these benefits:

- Individualized, differentiated writing practice

- Practice of new skills in the context of the writer's own work

- Opportunities for real revision and editing

- Fewer papers to grade

- Easy management

Independent Writing

The third component of the daily instructional model is independent writing. I've found that to maximize their learning, students need to write independently for an extended period of time, every single day. Research supports this conclusion. Donald Graves (1994), probably the most influential writer and researcher about writing instruction in our time, says:

> If students are not engaged in writing at least four days out of the week, and for a period of thirty-five to forty minutes, beginning in first grade, they will have little opportunity to learn to think through the medium of writing. . . . Students from another language or culture, or those who feel they have little to say, are particularly affected by [a] limited amount of time for writing. (p. 104)

During that time, students should be working on one or two extended pieces of writing each grading period that require them to use all their newly acquired and established trait-focused skills and apply all steps in the writing process: prewriting, drafting, sharing and feedback, revising, editing, and finishing or publishing.

Ideas for these pieces can come from the curriculum or from the students themselves, and they should explore each of the modes: narrative, informational/explanatory, and argument. Students need experience in all three to demonstrate skill for the different purposes for which they write, both in and out of school. It is interesting to note that as students become more skilled in each mode, they draw on other modes to make it stronger. For example, a writer might relate an anecdote (narrative mode) or provide information (informational/explanatory mode) within a piece of writing that is, overall, in the argument mode. Examples of writing that mix modes are important mentor texts as students come to this more complex understanding about the purposes for writing.

During independent writing, you should see teachers circulate around the room, stopping to talk to students who need support. They will be working in the writing workshop format: students are writing pieces they care about and are in different places in the writing process as they work with the ideas and take them to publication. Their conversations should be rich with language and suggestions of what to do next from the 4Ws: writing process, writing workshop, writing traits, and writing modes.

The Role of Formative Assessment

When students are ready to revise and then edit their work, the role of formative assessment becomes crystal clear. As opposed to its alter ego—summative large-scale assessment—formative classroom-based assessment serves as a guide for what lessons teachers present and how to nudge students forward with their pieces. The teacher's understanding of the writing process and the traits is critical as he or she guides students to the next steps.

Formative assessment can be thoughtful observations of students, or it may be more formal. A teacher may note that a student is having difficulty getting started and needs encouragement and an idea or two, or the student may be in the writing zone, and it's clear that the best thing to do is leave him or her alone to think and work. Formative assessment can also be an assessment of the writing using a scoring guide, so both teacher and students can see which areas are coming along and where they need to regroup and try something new. Formative assessment literally guides what teachers do to support student writers at every step along the way of the writing process. By bringing students into the assessment process and teaching them what to look for, the teacher empowers them to make good decisions about what to do next.

Trait-specific scoring guides like those found on pages 44 and 51, organized around the key qualities of each trait, give us the assessment needed to understand what students know and what they need to be taught. Assessment aligns perfectly with instruction when we use the key qualities of each trait, making it easy to see where students are succeeding and the specific areas where they need new instruction and support.

The practice of using assessment to guide instruction is a powerful tool in the writing classroom. The Carnegie report *Informing Writing: The Benefits of Formative Assessment* (Graham et al., 2011) provides empirical evidence of the transformative power of formative assessment:

"When teachers monitor students' progress, writing improves. When students evaluate their own writing, writing improves. When students receive feedback about their writing, writing improves. When students are partners in writing assessment, giving and receiving peer feedback, students' writing improves" (p. 27).

Knowing the Signs of an Effective Writing Classroom

Writing classrooms are dynamic places. Little stays the same from one day to the next. Any student may be horribly stuck one day and able to write his or her way out of the dilemma the next. To address the needs of every writer in the classroom, the teacher needs to have a deep commitment to teaching and applying writing skills using dynamic practices. To this end, teachers should do the following:

- Model and demonstrate with examples what they are hoping students will do and describe for them what it might look like in their minds as they are doing it

- Use resources, such as picture books or excerpts from chapters of young adult books, both fiction and nonfiction, as mentor texts for each of the traits and its key qualities

- Show students how to use all steps in the writing process to develop their writing over time

- Allow students choice about what they are writing

- Provide opportunities for short, midrange, and long-term writing assignments

- Develop an understanding of each mode of writing: narrative, informational/ explanatory, and argument

- Organize instruction around the key qualities of the traits, spiraling them across the year

- Provide meaningful feedback that validates what students are doing well, along with specific suggestions for improvement

- Monitor students' writing progress using the traits for formative assessment

- Be flexible

Writing Process: What to Look for, What to Say

As you go in and out of classrooms, notice if the writing process is clearly accessible to students in the form of a chart, poster, or other visual aid the teacher may have created. Look at the writing work of students posted around the room, and then follow up your observations with teachers.

- **Is the writing scripted, formulaic, and cookie-cutter?** Some writing assignments tend to produce text that is pretty much the same from one student to the next. Students complete the task, but they don't do the kind of thinking about writing that improves their skills over the long run.

Ask the teacher: "How did students choose their topics? Do you do a lot of prewriting with them? What are your favorite techniques?"

- **Do the pieces look different from one another?** Writing should be highly individual —some students will write longer and some shorter pieces. If students are allowed to choose their topics, they will invest more energy into writing them and create strong pieces.

Ask the teacher: "Did students have choices about what they wrote? Are there opportunities for them to take the piece in a different direction than other students?"

- **Is there evidence of the writing developing over time?** A strong writing program fosters the ability to work on a piece of writing over time, let it develop, and revise and edit it with guidance from peers and the teacher.

Ask the teacher: "How long did this piece take to develop? Did you confer with the student about the piece at any time and offer suggestions for revising and editing?"

- **Does the writing look cleanly edited?** Writing that is finished or published should be relatively clean of errors in conventions. Students should get the writing ready for the reader by checking each convention—spelling, capitalization, punctuation, grammar, and paragraphing—carefully.

Ask the teacher: "How do students learn to edit their own work? How much editing do you do for them? Are there specific skills you expect them to show mastery over and do independently?"

Writing Workshop: What to Look for, What to Say

Classroom management can be a challenge in a writing workshop, so as you look around the room, note the tools the teacher has created to support student independent work while he or she is circulating through the room to help students in one-on-one conferences. A schedule should be clearly posted to show how much time students should work on their writing and what meaningful alternative activities there are if they finish early. You should find students helping each other by reading and discussing their writing, based on one or more of the traits.

- **Are all students working on the same piece of writing?** If all students are working on the exact same piece of writing—a paragraph about pumpkins, for example—chances are they feel the teacher is looking for a "right" answer rather than feeling free to explore options that approach the topic in unique ways. For many students, this means the assignment becomes more about finishing and turning it in than doing the best they know how to do and asking for help to make it better. Choice is a big factor in student buy-in for the writing process and for doing the hard work it takes to improve.

Ask the teacher: "About how much of the time do students select their own topics?"

- **Are students at the same stage of the writing process?** Students should be in different places in their writing. Some may be drafting while others are revising or even editing, for that matter. In writing workshop, students should move through the writing process at their own pace with ample time for conferences with the teacher and peers to get feedback on their progress.

Ask the teacher: "How do students know it is time to move from one step of the writing process to the next? How do you monitor this process?"

- **Are teachers' comments—written on the student's paper or given in a conference—trait-specific and focused?** It's critical to know what to say to a student in writing or verbally. Specific, focused comments that validate what is done well and lead the student to understand what can improve, along with *how* to improve, help students begin to understand what revision is and why it is important.

Ask the teacher: "What do you write on student papers to let them know how they have done and what to revise or edit next? When you confer with students about their writing, what kind of comments do you offer for praise or improvement? Do you use the traits and their key qualities in these comments?"

- **Is it evident where students go in the classroom for help? What are the available resources to support them?** Books, papers, pens and pencils, computers, iPads, interactive whiteboard activities, and other writing resources should be clearly labeled and accessible for students.

Ask the teacher: "Where do students go for paper and resource materials when they write? Do you use technology for drafting or at any stage of the writing process?"

Writing Traits: What to Look for, What to Say

Trait posters either created by students or purchased commercially should be hanging in the classroom to use as resources. See if the posters include the four key qualities for each trait. You may notice student writing that has teacher comments about one or more traits. Or you may see notes by students themselves about the traits on their drafts. Again, follow up your observations with questions for teachers.

- **Is there evidence of the traits in the writing classroom?** Scoring guides for the teacher and student, writing folders, and posters help infuse the writing classroom with trait language. Trait terminology should permeate the writing classroom through resources that are readily available.

Ask the teacher: "Where do students go to find their student-friendly scoring guides? Where do you keep trait-specific materials such as picture books and other mentor texts so students can use them as models?"

- **Are student papers assessed using the traits?** Assessing student writing using one or more of the traits is the best way to learn the traits. When teachers get inside the writing, they understand how writing works, what students understand, and what they still need help to learn.

  Ask the teacher: "How often do you assess student writing for all the traits? Do you ever assess for just one trait at a time? How do you decide which one?"

- **Are there focus lessons about the key qualities of each trait?** Breaking each trait down into key qualities and spiraling those key qualities into instruction units over the year is a way to make teaching specific and comprehensive. Each key quality should be the focus of instruction for about a week; then teachers should move on.

  Ask the teacher: "How often do you focus lessons on each of the key qualities for the traits? How do you decide which one to cover next? About how long do you spend on a key quality before moving on to the next?"

- **Are students using writing folders?** Instead of worksheets—which should be banished—students should have a writing folder with two to four pieces of their work. Allowing them to practice in the context of their own work this way is a research-based practice. The folders should be dedicated only for this purpose and should not be a place where other materials reside.

  Ask the teacher: "Are you using writing folders with students? How often do students work with the pieces in the folder? When do you gather the pieces for the folder, and when do you choose one to finalize and turn in?"

Writing Modes: What to Look for, What to Say

Look for evidence that students have been producing work in different modes throughout the year. If student work is hanging on the wall, note which mode it is in and comment on the variety you find. Posters and other resources about modes should be easily visible so students can refer to them as they write. Refer to the Teacher-Friendly Scoring Guides for the writing modes (pages 79–81) as you evaluate the student work and formulate questions for teachers.

- **Does the teacher talk about the different purposes for writing as students begin to figure out what they want to say?** The modes are the overarching umbrella for writing that sets the course for the piece. There is content knowledge about each mode that students need to learn. For example, students learn that the organizational structure of narrative writing is usually chronological.

  Ask the teacher:"How do you help students understand the role of purpose in their writing? Do you show them models of what strong writing in each of the modes looks like before they begin?"

- **Can students explain the purpose for their writing?** Knowing the reason for writing (narrative, informational/explanatory, or argument) can open the door to strong first drafts. Asking students to explain the purpose for their writing will reveal how much they understand about the choice they made when they began or if they are simply doing the task because they were told to and haven't given the purpose much thought.

Ask the teacher: "How many times a year do students write an extended piece in the narrative mode? The informational/explanatory? The argument mode?"

- **Does the teacher show students how modes appear in printed materials, such as books read aloud or a textbook they read on their own?** Clearly, the writer must have one mode in mind as the purpose for the writing, but it can include passages that are in other modes to strengthen the piece overall.

Ask the teacher: "What have you found that helps students understand that different modes of writing often work together within one text? For example, how does a short anecdote make an argumentative essay stronger, or how can specific, accurate information add needed substance to narrative writing? Do you have models you've gathered to show students how mixing modes can make the purpose for their writing that much clearer?"

- **Are there posters or charts for students to refer to that relate to the modes?** As students take on more and more responsibility for their topics and purposes for writing, it is helpful for them to see reminders of options. Charts and posters hanging around the room are useful for teaching and for students to refer to as they work independently.

Ask the teacher: "Where would students go to find help writing in the modes? Do you use anchor charts to support your teaching in the modes?"

In the next chapter, you'll find an explanation of the scoring guides for traits as well as sample papers that have been assessed with the guides. You will also find a step-by-step protocol to follow in order to practice assessing these and other papers from classrooms in your school as you become more confident about the traits.

FOUR

ASSESSING STUDENT WRITING

Learning how to assess writing and get inside, dig around, kick the tires, is how teachers learn to teach writing. . . . You can't begin with lessons; you have to begin with assessment. Without the assessment, how do teachers know which lessons to teach? If you've ever sat in on a six-traits scoring session, you feel the energy and hear the "ahas" by every single person. It's powerful; it's transformative; it's magic.

—Gaye Lantz, Director of Curriculum, American
International School of Lagos, Nigeria

Practice makes perfect. And practice is how the traits become clear in the reader's mind. So in this chapter, you'll find examples of scored sample papers to study and try your own hand at assessing. I've included the scores the piece would receive as well as where to focus instructional attention next. I've also decided to focus on sentence fluency in each example, so you can see how traits "scale up" over the years.

You'll find one scored paper each for grades 1, 4, and 7.

Choosing the Right Scoring Guide

Beginning writers strive to master the basics of spacing, letter formation, upper- and lowercase letters, words, phrases and clauses, and finally sentences. As they develop these basic writing skills, they use pictures and traditional writing to capture the richness of their ideas, form the organizational structure, and reach out to the reader with voice. Teachers should assess these writers using the Teacher-Friendly Scoring Guide for Beginning Writers (page 44), generally a good match for grades K–2.

Students who are writing a paragraph—three or more sentences on the same topic, clustered together—are no longer beginning writers. They have the basics under control and are now attempting to write longer texts with increasing complexity. Writers at this stage of development should be assessed by their teachers using the Teacher-Friendly Scoring Guide for Established Writers (page 51), generally a good match for grades 3–8 and above.

After you assess the piece for the trait, regardless of the age of the writer, you may want to use the Teacher-Friendly Scoring Guides for the modes as well (pages 79–81). These guides provide a holistic response to how well the writer fulfilled the purpose of the writing: narrative, informational/explanatory, or argument.

In addition to what teachers need to assess writing, there are student-friendly scoring guides that will allow students to self-assess and monitor their own writing progress. For beginning writers, generally in grades K–2, the Student-Friendly Scoring Guide for Beginning Writers (page 58) uses pictures and simple language to convey conceptual understanding and works well for readers who are not reading independently. More accomplished writers should use the Student-Friendly Scoring Guide for Established Writers A (page 65) or B (page 72). The first is well suited to grades 3–5 and the second for middle school and above.

Teachers should match the scoring guide and the information it provides to the developmental readiness of the writer in order to nudge the writer forward in writing in each trait. Encourage teachers not to be locked into a grade level or age but to think about what information will be most helpful to the writer.

The scoring guides are a key part of the feedback cycle to students, but for an accurate and reliable rating, two other elements are needed: (1) models at each grade level that show what is typical for high to low scores in each of the modes and (2) practice using the scoring guide with at least twenty-five papers before scoring "live" samples.

Let's get started by establishing a procedure and test-driving the trait-based writing scoring guide.

Step-by-Step Assessment

Gather the sample papers you wish to assess—either the ones provided on pages 38–42 or a handful from your school at different grade levels—and follow these steps. You'll feel slow and a bit awkward when assessing at first; you'll be going through seven pages of trait-specific criteria after all, and that is a lot at the beginning. But you'll get faster and faster as you go and as you become familiar with the language that defines each trait at different levels of performance. Before long, you'll be able to read and assess a paper every two to three minutes—for all the traits. Seriously!

You may want to have a partner to talk with as you try your hand with the scoring guide. Most beginners with trait-based assessment find it useful to go over what they notice in the student writing with someone else as they are reading and thinking. This also builds confidence that you can do this task fairly easily and with reliability.

Use the scoring guide that matches the grade levels of the papers you're assessing (pages 44–57 and at **go.solution-tree.com/leadership**). Then follow these steps to assess the papers for one or more traits:

1. Read the descriptors for each of the three performance levels (figure 4.1, page 38). For example, for the established writer's scoring guide, they are:

   - High—6 (exceptional) and 5 (strong)

   - Middle—4 (refining) and 3 (developing)

   - Low—2 (emerging) and 1 (rudimentary)

2. Read one of the student papers carefully. As tempting as it might be, avoid skimming and scanning. Even the most experienced reader is surprised now and again.

3. Assess the paper for one or more traits, assigning a score of 1 to 6 based on the criteria in the guide. Begin by targeting the zone the paper is in—*low, middle,* or *high*—and select the key qualities that match the paper at that level. To verify, check the wording of the key qualities descriptions preceding or following the zone you've selected to make sure you have chosen the most accurate match. Some papers, for instance, may be in the middle for three key qualities but high in the other one. That would mean the paper would receive a 4 in that trait, the higher side of the middle range.

4. Repeat the process of matching the zone (low, middle, or high) and the key qualities to the paper and reading above and below to validate the score. Select the overall score, 1 to 6, for each trait that best matches the number of key qualities in each zone and where the others lie, either higher or lower. Some people find it useful to highlight or checkmark the key qualities in each zone as they make a match. At the end, then, they can look over each trait and determine the final score.

After you assess the piece for the trait, regardless of the age of the writer, you may want to use the Teacher-Friendly Scoring Guides for the modes as well. These guides provide a holistic response to how well the writer fulfilled the purpose of the writing: narrative, informational/explanatory, or argument. In general, figure 4.1 (page 38) shows how the scores at each point on the scale should be conceived.

> **6 Exceptional**—The piece exceeds expectations in this trait. It really works well. There is no need for revision or editing unless the writer wants to push further into new territory.
>
> **5 Strong**—The piece stands on its own. It may need a bit of revision or editing but nothing the writer can't handle on his or her own.
>
> **4 Refining**—The piece has more strengths than weaknesses in the trait. A moderate amount of revision and editing is needed. Papers that score a 4 are often considered "proficient," which means they meet most state and local standards.
>
> **3 Developing**—The piece has slightly more weaknesses than strengths in this trait. Some revision and editing are needed throughout.
>
> **2 Emerging**—The piece hints at what the writer might do with the trait. Extensive revision and editing are required.
>
> **1 Rudimentary**—The piece does not contain the core features of any of the key qualities for this trait. The writer may wish to start over or abandon the piece completely.

Figure 4.1: The scoring guides' six performance levels.

Let's look at sample assessments of student writing from grades 1, 4, and 7. Note that because the papers are not final polished pieces of writing meant to be read by an outside audience, the presentation trait has not been assessed.

Grade 1 Sample Assessment

The topic here is pretty standard for first grade—the life cycle of a butterfly (see figure 4.2). But the writer puts a delightful spin on it by writing, in a clear, chronological fashion, from the perspective of the insect. I applaud her organization. I also admire (ignoring the spelling) her combination of content words—such as *caterpillar, chrysalis,* and *butterfly*—and action phrases, such as *eat and eat, growing wings, break through,* and *pop.* The piece, however, contains many short, repetitive sentences that begin with *I.* So comments and suggestions are focused on sentence fluency.

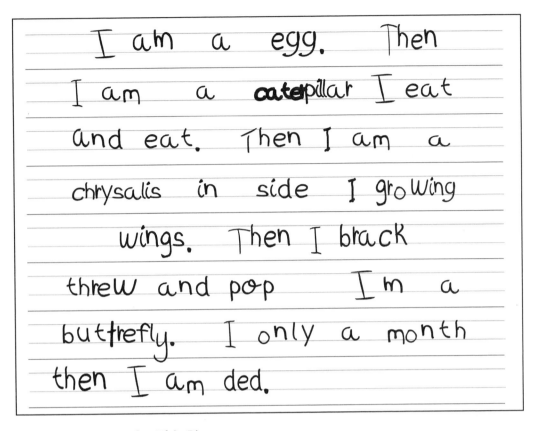

Scores for This Piece

Ideas: 5   Word Choice: 6
Organization: 5   Sentence Fluency: 3*
Voice: 4   Conventions: 5

* Trait for focus to improve on in a conference

Figure 4.2: A first grader's essay on the life cycle of a butterfly.

I learned so much about the life cycle of a butterfly from your piece. You start with birth and end with death. That is an extremely logical way to organize a piece of writing. Hooray! And I'm sure writing from the perspective of the butterfly enabled you to feel what being a butterfly might be like. That's hard to do, but you make it look easy. You've got some terrific words and phrases, such as *caterpillar*, *chrysalis*, and *butterfly*. You've also got some terrific sentences, such as "Then I break through and, pop, I'm a butterfly." Now, let's try to revise them so they are different, one to the next.

Grade 4 Sample Assessment

From a list of weather-forecasting tools, this student chose to become a digital thermometer and write a letter of application to a meteorologist explaining why he'd be the perfect hire (see figure 4.3, page 40).

Dear Fred Jones,
I am looking around town for a job. My name is Digital Thermometer. I am like a normal thermometer but I can do much, much more. I can tell you the high tempreture, low termpreture, maximum, medium, and minimum. I can't tell you how much I want this job. I promise you will get the weather right almost all the time. So if you hire me it will help the U.S.A. a whole lot! So if you hire me your life will be a whole lot better. Thank You so much.
                                        Sincerely,
                                        Digital Thermometer

Scores for This Piece

Ideas: 3	Word Choice: 3
Organization: 4	Sentence Fluency: 2*
Voice: 6	Conventions: 5

* Trait for focus to improve on in a conference

Figure 4.3: A fourth grader's essay—a digital thermometer applies for work.

The assignment is imaginative, and because his voice is strong, I sense the student enjoyed carrying it out. Voice is usually a reliable indicator of the student's interest and ownership in an assignment. The thermometer's pride in his unique skills and qualities rings out in the details of the piece. He makes a compelling argument, which is easy to follow because of his excellent use of conventions. However, although the sentences are mechanically correct, they lack variety. Notice that all but the last two are nearly identical in length and begin with the word *I*. Therefore, I'd again encourage work on sentence fluency, as in the following comments:

> Your piece has all the elements of a strong letter of application: you explain why you are writing, why you would be perfect for the job, and how you would improve the quality of life for your employer. Your message is persuasive, in other words, and that comes through in your voice. I sense you really want the job because of your voice. You deserve high marks for conventions, too. Your grammar and mechanics are, for the most part, perfect, which makes reading your writing a pleasure. One way you could improve your piece is to bring more sentence variety to it. Notice how almost every

one of your sentences is about the same length and begins with the word *I.* How about changing a few to add interest and create rhythm? Let's pick a few and get started.

Grade 7 Sample Assessment

This piece makes a strong case for the claim that Missouri has all the energy resources it needs without importing oil (figure 4.4).

To the editor,

Missouri needs to be energy independent. We have many alternative sources of energy, such as: bio diesel fuel, wind energy, and hydro electricity.

Missouri is an excellent position to produce bio-diesel fuel. In Missouri there are three major companies producing bio diesel fuel. Bio diesel is a totally renewable fuel source. It is also clean burning, non toxic and bio degradable. This alternative fuel source gives an additional market for Missouri farmers to sell their excess crops.

Northwest Missouri hosts many wind turbines. These are used to produce electricity. The town of Rock Port, Missouri, is the first town in America to be produce enough wind energy to meet 100% of the town's needs. Wind is very versatile. It can be used for several purposes such as pumping water, heating water, generating electricity. Because the wind blows strongest at night when the need for electricity is low, the excess electricity can be used in hydrogen production. This hydrogen can then be used to power fuel cells. This electricity can be used later when the demand is greater. Farmers and ranchers can also use small wind turbines to pump water for their livestock.

In Missouri we have many rivers and lakes which could be used for hydro electricity. Yet the Missouri river is not dammed in Missouri, there are five major dams along the Mississippi river. Those five dams produce an estimated 889,000 megawatt hours (mwh) per year. If we could capture half of that energy, it would be three times as much energy as we used in Missouri in all of 2004, which was 123,000 mwh. Missouri has the potential hydro-electric energy, now we need the power plants to harness it Also the only environmental problem would be to a few fish which would get sucked into the turbines.

With all these energy sources there is little to no reason we should need imported oil. We have all the energy sources we need. What we need now is the dedication and determination to use them.

Scores for This Piece

Ideas: 5	Word Choice: 4
Organization: 4	Sentence Fluency: 3*
Voice: 5	Conventions: 5

* Trait for focus to improve on in a conference.

Figure 4.4: A seventh grader's essay advocating energy independence for Missouri.

It would be helpful to know where the writer obtained the information and facts, and the teacher might push the student to add citations within the text. The sentences need the most work, however. They are correct but not terribly fluent. Many sentences begin with the same construction or are approximately the same length. There is little evidence that the writer "hears" the flow as he or she reads it back to him- or herself and makes adjustments.

It's important to focus comments in one area, so if sentence fluency was the target, the comments might read like this:

> You are developing a sense of fluency; to move it along, keep reading! Do you have a favorite author? Pay attention to the writer's use of sentence structures in each book or article that person has written. You might find some good tips for your own work as you examine the author's. To revise this piece, take some time to look at every single sentence, both individually and in relation to the surrounding sentences. Which sentence do you think is the strongest? Which is the most problematic? What is the difference between them? Can you rework your least favorites to include a sense of rhythm similar to the smooth sentences and passages? This might be a good activity to do with a peer who is having a similar problem. Read your choices aloud, together, and see what your ear tells you about the sentences.

Grading

Once the assessment is complete, you and the teachers will be able to look at the scores and determine which traits a student is handling well and which need the most time and attention. This is the fundamental purpose of formative assessment. Teachers may want to record these scores in their gradebooks to document progress. Have them add up the number of points earned out of the total possible. Teachers can use the reproducible grading chart (page 82) to figure out a final grade for the piece. Whether the piece is scored in one or seven traits, the chart provides a percentage equivalent that can then be turned into a grade based on the scale used in your school. If the piece is scored for the mode as well, suggest to teachers that they skip the presentation trait and substitute the mode score, since the chart allows for up to seven scores.

A Preview of the Common Core Writing Assessments

At this book's time of printing, the CCSS sample assessments were just that—samples of what the final assessments may contain. We do know there will be formative, interim, and summative assessments at different times during the year, all of which will be based on dynamic writing practices rather than out-of-context prompts. Throughout the sample assessments provided by Partnership for Assessment of Readiness for College and Careers (PARCC) and the Smarter Balanced Assessment Consortium (SBAC), students are asked to write for a wide variety of purposes and in many learning contexts. For example, in the practice ELA test items posted online by SBAC (2012) for grade 5 practice in writing, students are asked to write an opinion piece based on reading passages that require them to incorporate the traits:

Your Assignment

The legislature has passed a new law that allows only service dogs to go with their owners into public places. You are working on the school newsletter, and you have been asked to write a multiparagraph article giving your opinion on the new law. In your article, you will take a side as to whether you think allowing only service dogs in public places is a good law or whether other service animals should also be permitted. Your article will be read by the teachers and students at your school. In your article, clearly state your opinion and support your opinion with reasons that are thoroughly developed using information from what you have read and viewed.

REMEMBER: A well-written opinion article:

- Has a clear opinion
- Is well-organized and stays on the topic
- Has an introduction and a conclusion
- Uses transitions
- Uses details from the sources to support your opinion
- Develops ideas clearly
- Uses clear language
- Follows rules of writing (spelling, punctuation, and grammar)

The ideas, organization, word choice, traits, and key qualities are clearly called into action here, as is the razor-sharp attention to the purpose: stating an opinion. It seems apparent from these early indicators that the Common Core assessments will use scoring guides that address the mode of writing along with the traits. By working with modes and traits, teachers can help students prepare for these important assessments, regardless of their final form.

Assessment can be a powerful way to inform teachers and staff about how the writing program is working at your school, too. In the next chapter, you'll learn how to assess your school on a continuum of writing instruction designed to focus on professional growth. We'll explore next steps to take with the staff as a whole, as well as with individual teachers who are looking for guidance on how to improve.

Teacher-Friendly Scoring Guide for Beginning Writers

Use this scoring guide for writers as they strive to master the basics of spacing, letter formation, upper- and lowercase letters, words, phrases, and clauses, sentences, and conventions: spelling, capitalization, punctuation, paraphrasing, and grammar and usage (generally K–2).

Ideas

The piece's content—the central message and the details that support that message

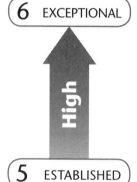

6 EXCEPTIONAL

5 ESTABLISHED

A. **Finding a big idea:** The writer shows understanding of the topic through personal experience or research. The big idea is clear, coherent, and original.

B. **Focusing on the big idea:** The writer gets at the heart of the topic and writes about it using original and complex thinking. The big idea is narrow and specific.

C. **Staying with the big idea:** The writer creates meaning for the reader by elaborating with details that develop the big idea. Pictures (if present) enhance that idea but aren't necessary for comprehension.

D. **Using juicy details:** The writer anticipates what the reader might want to know by providing details that clarify the big idea. He or she has carefully selected details to create meaning for the reader and show what is important.

4 EXTENDING

3 EXPANDING

A. **Finding a big idea:** The writer explains a simple idea or tells a simple story with words and pictures. His or her topic is clear but may not be original.

B. **Focusing on the big idea:** The writer remains true to his or her topic but in a general way. His or her piece may be too broad, fuzzy, or predictable.

C. **Staying with the big idea:** The writer offers clear thinking, but the information he or she provides is incomplete or irrelevant. He or she fails to flesh out the big idea or veers into a new topic without realizing it.

D. **Using juicy details:** The writer provides details, though not consistently. He or she settles for the simplest way to convey information or tell the story, rather than reaching for details that create a clear picture in the reader's mind.

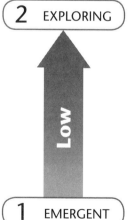

2 EXPLORING

1 EMERGENT

A. **Finding a big idea:** The writer conveys little information in text or pictures; at most, only the beginning of an idea comes through. An oral reading by the writer is needed to identify the topic.

B. **Focusing on the big idea:** The writer provides text, pictures, and other elements that are so unrecognizable or random that the reader can't pinpoint the big idea. What matters to the writer about this topic is not clear.

C. **Staying with the big idea:** The writer does not extend a clear message. Letter strings indicate that he or she is trying to express something about the topic, but the reader cannot discern precisely what it is.

D. **Using juicy details:** The writer must read his or her writing aloud and explain the drawings for the reader to understand what he or she has to say about the topic. He or she has left many of the reader's questions unanswered.

page 1 of 7

Organization

The internal structure of the piece—the thread of logic and the pattern of meaning

6 EXCEPTIONAL

5 ESTABLISHED

High

A. **Starting with a bold beginning:** The writer provides an original beginning. He or she tries to grab the reader's attention right off the bat.

B. **Creating a mighty middle:** The writer presents at least one well-developed paragraph. He or she elaborates on ideas and connects one idea to the next, using sophisticated sequence and transition words: *later, otherwise, either.*

C. **Finishing with an excellent ending:** The writer ends the piece in a logical place. He or she tries to wrap up all the loose ends and give the reader something to think about.

D. **Adding a terrific title:** The writer provides a title that captures the piece's big idea. He or she has put a lot of thought into the title.

4 EXTENDING

3 EXPANDING

Middle

A. **Starting with a bold beginning:** The writer provides a clear beginning, but it is predictable: "Once upon a time," "One time," "First," or something along those lines.

B. **Creating a mighty middle:** The writer presents two or more sentences on the topic—the beginning of a paragraph—that contain a few standard sequence and transition words: *first, next, but.* Or, he or she presents one sentence and pictures that develop the big idea.

C. **Finishing with an excellent ending:** The writer provides a pat summary: "The end," "Thank you," "That's it." He or she seems to have run out of steam and chooses the easy way out.

D. **Adding a terrific title:** The writer provides a title, but it's just a word or key phrase. It's generic and would work for almost anyone's paper on this topic.

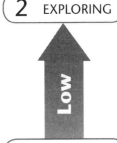

2 EXPLORING

1 EMERGENT

Low

A. **Starting with a bold beginning:** The writer doesn't provide a clear beginning. He or she has simply filled the page with letters, words, and/or pictures in no particular order.

B. **Creating a mighty middle:** The writer presents text that contains letters, words, or approximations of both but no sentences. He or she does not attempt to coordinate written elements.

C. **Finishing with an excellent ending:** The writer has given no thought to how the piece ends. There is no sense of closure; the piece simply stops.

D. **Adding a terrific title:** The writer provides no title at all or, at most, a title that gives no indication of what the piece is about: "My paper," "Writing," or his or her name.

Voice

The tone and tenor of the piece—the personal stamp of the writer, which is achieved through a strong understanding of purpose and audience

6 EXCEPTIONAL

A. **Expressing a feeling:** The writer expresses a distinct tone—bittersweet, compassionate, funny, frustrated, scared, and so on. He or she uses language that speaks to the intended audience.

B. **Communicating with sparkle and pizzazz:** The writer takes real risks to create a truly individual piece of writing. He or she has found an original way to address the topic and satisfy the reader.

C. **Reaching out to the reader:** The writer is mindful of the audience and connects purposefully to the audience. Clearly, it matters to the writer that the reader gets it.

5 ESTABLISHED

D. **Saying things in new ways:** The writer expresses him- or herself in unique ways. He or she owns the topic by addressing the big idea behind it distinctively.

4 EXTENDING

A. **Expressing a feeling:** The writer expresses a tone, but it's general—happy, sad, or mad. Oversized letters, exclamation points, underlining, repetition, and pictures are used for emphasis.

B. **Communicating with sparkle and pizzazz:** The writer offers a fresh word, interesting image, and/or unusual detail here and there. But, for the most part, he or she uses routine language.

C. **Reaching out to the reader:** The writer connects with the reader intermittently. He or she only allows a sneak peek into what matters or is interesting to him or her.

3 EXPANDING

D. **Saying things in new ways:** The writer approaches the topic predictably. What he or she thinks or feels about the big idea shows up in pictures or in an occasional colorful word or phrase.

2 EXPLORING

A. **Expressing a feeling:** The writer doesn't express a tone. He or she has not provided any evidence of how he or she feels about the topic.

B. **Communicating with sparkle and pizzazz:** The writer offers "Plain Jane" letters, words, and/or sentences. The writing feels like it came off an assembly line.

C. **Reaching out to the reader:** The writer provides no evidence that he or she has considered the audience; the writing may be copied from another source. He or she writes generically about the topic.

1 EMERGENT

D. **Saying things in new ways:** The writer's work lacks a point of view. He or she produces drawings and/or writing that feels forced, as if responding to a simple question.

Word Choice

The specific vocabulary the writer uses to convey meaning and enlighten the reader

6 EXCEPTIONAL

High

5 ESTABLISHED

A. **Choosing zippy verbs:** The writer uses action words effectively—verbs that add energy to the writing.

B. **Picking "just right" words:** The writer selects words with care and intent. Places in the writing catch the reader's attention because the words or phrases work so well.

C. **Stretching for never-before-tried words:** The writer tries words that are new to him or her because they communicate precisely what he or she is trying to say. He or she doesn't settle for the first word that comes to mind.

D. **Using words to create meaning:** The writer uses everyday words well—words that are correct, colorful, and creative. He or she may even have tried using figurative language, such as metaphors and alliteration.

4 EXTENDING

Middle

3 EXPANDING

A. **Choosing zippy verbs:** The writer uses verbs correctly but doesn't choose zippy ones. He or she may use forms of "to be" almost exclusively.

B. **Picking "just right" words:** The writer offers only one or two moments that sparkle or show precision. Most of the words and phrases are basic and unoriginal.

C. **Stretching for never-before-tried words:** The writer seems comfortable with the first word that comes to mind. He or she makes no attempt to draw from the large bank of words in his or her vocabulary.

D. **Using words to create meaning:** The writer uses ordinary and/or imprecise words to explain or tell, making it hard for the reader to get a clear picture of what he or she is trying to convey. Occasional misused words bog down the reader.

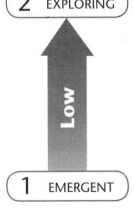

2 EXPLORING

Low

1 EMERGENT

A. **Choosing zippy verbs:** The writer seems confused about how to apply verbs. He or she neglects to use them, or uses them incorrectly, in places where they could be effective.

B. **Picking "just right" words:** The writer is trying to create words but with very limited success. He or she is only writing simple words, which at times are lost in a string of letters.

C. **Stretching for never-before-tried words:** The writer uses only words he or she knows—names, simple high-frequency words, words around the room, and so on. Few words are original.

D. **Using words to create meaning:** The writer uses words that are obvious choices such as labels on pictures or key names or places. Readers are challenged to understand the words because there are standard and nonstandard letters throughout.

What Principals Need to Know About Teaching and Learning Writing © 2014 Solution Tree Press • solution-tree.com
Visit **go.solution-tree.com/leadership** to download this page.

Sentence Fluency

The way the words and phrases flow through the piece—the auditory trait, because it's "read" with the ear as much as the eye

6 EXCEPTIONAL

High

5 ESTABLISHED

A. **Building complete sentences:** The writer crafts solid sentences throughout the piece—sentences that are varied and grammatically correct. Any fragments add to the flow of the piece.

B. **Starting sentences in different ways:** The writer begins sentences differently. If any sentences begin the same way, it is a deliberate move to create a pleasing rhythm.

C. **Varying sentence lengths:** The writer creates sentences of various lengths. Some are short, some are long, and some are in between; the variety enhances the piece's fluency.

D. **Making smooth-sounding sentences:** The writer creates sentences that flow together smoothly. He or she may use conjunctions to connect ideas and make the piece a breeze to read aloud.

4 EXTENDING

Middle

3 EXPANDING

A. **Building complete sentences:** The writer offers simple, grammatically correct sentences, with a few exceptions. Fragments, if present, are unintentional or ineffective, which disrupts the piece's flow.

B. **Starting sentences in different ways:** The writer begins sentences the same way, for the most part. Only a couple of sentences begin differently from the rest.

C. **Varying sentence lengths:** The piece contains short sentences of almost equal length or, perhaps, one or two extremely long sentences that go on seemingly endlessly.

D. **Making smooth-sounding sentences:** The writer uses simple conjunctions (*and, or, but*) to connect ideas and make sentences flow. Despite a few awkward moments, the piece can be read aloud without too much trouble.

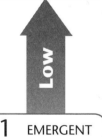

2 EXPLORING

Low

1 EMERGENT

A. **Building complete sentences:** The writer struggles with sentence construction. There are no correctly formed sentences in the piece, only short or repetitive words and phrases.

B. **Starting sentences in different ways:** The writer begins each line in much the same way. Repeating words and phrases make reading a challenge.

C. **Varying sentence lengths:** The writer puts words down but without much regard to how they sound together. Some words stand alone.

D. **Making smooth-sounding sentences:** The writer must read the piece aloud for the reader to hear how the words flow. Only the writer can read the piece with any sense of continuity.

Conventions

The mechanical correctness of the piece—correct use of conventions (spelling, capitalization, punctuation, paragraphing, and grammar and usage), which guides the reader through the text easily

6 EXCEPTIONAL

High

5 ESTABLISHED

A. **Spelling well:** The writer spells high-frequency words correctly and other types of words phonetically (*ardvrk*). The spelling doesn't impede the reader.

B. **Capitalizing correctly:** The writer applies basic capitalization rules with consistency, such as beginning sentences and proper names with a capital letter and always capitalizing the pronoun *I*.

C. **Punctuating powerfully:** The writer uses punctuation marks correctly to guide the reader. He or she may also try to use them creatively to emphasize points and enhance fluency.

D. **Applying basic grammar:** The writer shows control over basic Standard English grammar. He or she applies usage rules consistently and accurately.

4 EXTENDING

Middle

3 EXPANDING

A. **Spelling well:** The writer spells simple high-frequency words correctly or phonetically (such as *kttn*, *sed*, and *wnt*), making them easy to read. More sophisticated words present a challenge, however.

B. **Capitalizing correctly:** The writer is unpredictable when it comes to capitalization. He or she may begin some sentences with a capital, for instance, or only occasionally capitalize the pronoun *I*.

C. **Punctuating powerfully:** The writer uses end punctuation marks more of the time. There is little evidence in the piece of control over punctuation.

D. **Applying basic grammar:** The writer uses Standard English grammar inconsistently. He or she attempts to apply rules correctly but misses the mark as many times as he or she hits it.

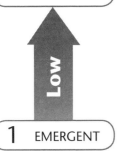

2 EXPLORING

Low

1 EMERGENT

A. **Spelling well:** The writer uses letter strings and prephonetic spelling (such as *gGmkRt*). The words are not spelled correctly.

B. **Capitalizing correctly:** The writer shows no control over the use of capitals. Capital letters are randomly placed throughout the piece.

C. **Punctuating powerfully:** The writer rarely uses punctuation. When he or she does use it, it's applied incorrectly.

D. **Applying basic grammar:** The writer has generated so little text it is difficult to determine what he or she knows about grammar and usage. When the writer reads the piece aloud, however, grammar and usage issues reveal themselves.

Presentation

The physical appearance of the piece, which, when visually appealing, provides a welcome mat and invites the reader in

6 EXCEPTIONAL

High

5 ESTABLISHED

A. **Forming letters correctly:** The writer correctly forms letters throughout the piece. Both upper- and lowercase letters are written clearly.

B. **Printing words neatly:** The writer is careful to apply the right amount of pressure to create letters that are uniform and pleasing to the eye.

C. **Putting spaces between letters and words:** The writer uses spacing correctly and consistently. Spaces between letters and words are even and make the piece easy to read.

D. **Turning in a tidy final piece:** The writer has made sure that the piece's overall appearance is inviting to the reader. It's neat.

4 EXTENDING

Middle

3 EXPANDING

A. **Forming letters correctly:** The writer forms some letters using proper form, including upper- and lowercase letters. But there is inconsistency in the way those letters are formed.

B. **Printing words neatly:** The writer creates letters that slant in every direction. He or she may apply too much pressure or not enough, making the letters too bold or too light to read easily.

C. **Putting spaces between letters and words:** The writer puts spaces between letters and words, but the amount of space is uneven. Some letters and words sit very close to one another, making them difficult to read.

D. **Turning in a tidy final piece:** The writer has not sufficiently polished the piece's appearance. The piece may have a few cross-outs or smudges. It may be wrinkled or torn at the corner. It's readable but not neat.

2 EXPLORING

Low

1 EMERGENT

A. **Forming letters correctly:** The writer forms letters randomly. There appears to be no intentional use of upper- and lowercase letters.

B. **Printing words neatly:** The writer puts his or her thoughts down hastily and with little care. Pictures are drawn and letters are formed haphazardly.

C. **Putting spaces between letters and words:** The writer has not used spacing effectively at all. Letters, words, and pictures are jumbled together.

D. **Turning in a tidy final piece:** The writer has written so carelessly that the piece is almost illegible. It contains many cross-outs, smudges, wrinkles, tears, folds, and so forth.

Source: Reprinted with permission of Scholastic, Inc.

Teacher-Friendly Scoring Guide for Established Writers

Use this trait-based analytical scoring guide for writers who can generate enough text to write a paragraph to those who can write full-blown essays, stories, and research reports. This scoring guide can be used with writers at any age, but it generally applies to grades 3 and up.

Ideas

The piece's content—its central message and the details that support that message

A. **Finding a topic:** The writer offers a clear, central theme or a simple, original story line that is memorable.

B. **Focusing the topic:** The writer narrows the theme or story line to create a piece that is clear, tight, and manageable.

C. **Developing the topic:** The writer provides enough critical evidence to support the theme and shows insight on the topic. Or, he or she tells the story in a fresh way through an original, unpredictable plot.

D. **Using details:** The writer offers credible, accurate details that create pictures in the reader's mind, from the beginning of the piece to the end. Those details provide the reader with evidence of the writer's knowledge about or experience with the topic.

A. **Finding a topic:** The writer offers a recognizable but broad theme or story line. He or she stays on topic but in a predictable way.

B. **Focusing the topic:** The writer needs to crystallize his or her topic around the central theme or story line. He or she does not focus on a specific aspect of the topic.

C. **Developing the topic:** The writer draws on personal knowledge and experience but does not offer a unique perspective. He or she does not probe deeply but instead gives the reader only a glimpse at aspects of the topic.

D. **Using details:** The writer offers details, but they do not always hit the mark because they are inaccurate or irrelevant. He or she does not create a picture in the reader's mind because key questions about the central theme or story line have not been addressed.

A. **Finding a topic:** The writer has not settled on a topic and, therefore, may offer only a series of unfocused, repetitious, or random thoughts.

B. **Focusing the topic:** The writer has not narrowed his or her topic in a meaningful way. It's hard to tell what the writer thinks is important since he or she devotes equal importance to each piece of information.

C. **Developing the topic:** The writer has created a piece that is so short, the reader cannot fully understand or appreciate what he or she wants to say. He or she may have simply restated an assigned topic or responded to a prompt without devoting much thought or effort to it.

D. **Using details:** The writer has clearly devoted little attention to details. The writing contains limited or completely inaccurate information. After reading the piece, the reader is left with many unanswered questions.

page 1 of 7

Organization

The internal structure of the piece—the thread of logic and the pattern of meaning

6 EXCEPTIONAL

A. **Creating the lead:** The writer grabs the reader's attention from the start and leads him or her into the piece naturally. He or she entices the reader, providing a tantalizing glimpse of what is to come.

B. **Using sequence words and transition words:** The writer includes a variety of carefully selected sequence words (*later, then, meanwhile*) and transition words (*however, also, clearly*), which are placed wisely to guide the reader through the piece by showing how ideas progress, relate, and/or diverge.

C. **Structuring the body:** The writer creates a piece that is easy to follow by fitting details together logically. He or she slows down to spotlight important points or events and speeds up when he or she needs to move the reader along.

D. **Ending with a sense of resolution:** The writer sums up his or her thinking in a natural, thoughtful, and convincing way. He or she anticipates and answers any lingering questions the reader may have, providing a strong sense of closure.

5 STRONG

4 REFINING

A. **Creating the lead:** The writer presents an introduction, although it may not be original or thought provoking. Instead, it may be a simple restatement of the topic and, therefore, does not create a sense of anticipation about what is to come.

B. **Using sequence words and transition words:** The writer uses sequence words to show the logical order of details, but they feel obvious or canned. The use of transition words is spotty and rarely creates coherence.

C. **Structuring the body:** The writer sequences events and important points logically, for the most part. However, the reader may wish to move a few things around to create a more sensible flow. He or she may also feel the urge to speed up or slow down for more satisfying pacing.

D. **Ending with a sense of resolution:** The writer ends the piece on a familiar note: "Thank you for reading . . .," "Now you know all about . . .," or "They lived happily ever after." He or she needs to tie up loose ends to leave the reader with a sense of satisfaction or closure.

3 DEVELOPING

2 EMERGING

A. **Creating the lead:** The writer does not give the reader any clue about what is to come. The opening point feels as if it were chosen randomly.

B. **Using sequence words and transition words:** The writer does not provide sequence and /or transition words between sections or provides words that are so confusing the reader is unable to sort one section from another.

C. **Structuring the body:** The writer does not show clearly what comes first, next, and last, making it difficult to understand how sections fit together. The writer slows down when he or she should speed up and speeds up when he or she should slow down.

D. **Ending with a sense of resolution:** The writer ends the piece with no conclusion at all—or nothing more than "The End" or something equally bland. There is no sense of resolution, no sense of completion.

1 RUDIMENTARY

page 2 of 7

Voice

The tone and tenor of the piece—the personal stamp of the writer, which is achieved through a strong understanding of purpose and audience

6 EXCEPTIONAL

High

5 STRONG

A. **Establishing a tone:** The writer cares about the topic, and it shows. The writing is expressive and compelling. The reader feels the writer's conviction, authority, and integrity.

B. **Conveying the purpose:** The writer makes clear his or her reason for creating the piece. He or she offers a point of view that is appropriate for the mode (narrative, informational/explanatory, or argument), which compels the reader to read on.

C. **Creating a connection to the audience:** The writer speaks in a way that makes the reader want to listen. He or she has considered what the reader needs to know and the best way to convey it by sharing his or her fascination, feelings, and opinions about the topic.

D. **Taking risks to create voice:** The writer expresses ideas in new ways, which makes the piece interesting and original. The writing sounds like the writer because of his or her use of distinctive, just-right words and phrases.

4 REFINING

Middle

3 DEVELOPING

A. **Establishing a tone:** The writer has established a tone that can be described as "pleasing" or "sincere" but not "passionate" or "compelling." He or she attempts to create a tone that hits the mark, but the overall result feels generic.

B. **Conveying the purpose:** The writer has chosen a voice for the piece that is not completely clear. There are only a few moments when the reader understands where the writer is coming from and why he or she wrote the piece.

C. **Creating a connection to the audience:** The writer keeps the reader at a distance. The connection between reader and writer is tenuous because the writer reveals little about what is important or meaningful about the topic.

D. **Taking risks to create voice:** The writer creates a few moments that catch the reader's attention, but only a few. The piece sounds like anyone could have written it. It lacks the energy, commitment, and conviction that would distinguish it from other pieces on the same topic.

2 EMERGING

Low

1 RUDIMENTARY

A. **Establishing a tone:** The writer has produced a lifeless piece—one that is monotonous, mechanical, repetitious, and/or off-putting to the reader.

B. **Conveying the purpose:** The writer chose the topic for mysterious reasons. The piece may be filled with random thoughts, technical jargon, or inappropriate vocabulary, making it impossible to discern how the writer feels about the topic.

C. **Creating a connection to the audience:** The writer provides no evidence that he or she has considered what the reader might need to know to connect with the topic. Or there is an obvious mismatch between the piece's tone and the intended audience.

D. **Taking risks to create voice:** The writer creates no highs and lows. The piece is flat and lifeless, causing the reader to wonder why the writer wrote it in the first place. The writer's voice does not pop out, even for a moment.

page 3 of 7

Word Choice

The specific vocabulary the writer uses to convey meaning and enlighten the reader

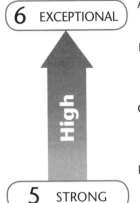

A. **Applying strong verbs:** The writer uses many action words, giving the piece punch and pizzazz. He or she has stretched to find lively verbs that add energy to the piece.

B. **Selecting striking words and phrases:** The writer uses many finely honed words and phrases. His or her creative and effective use of literary techniques such as alliteration, simile, and metaphor makes the piece a pleasure to read.

C. **Using specific and accurate words:** The writer uses words with precision. He or she selects words the reader needs to fully understand the message. The writer chooses nouns, adjectives, adverbs, and so forth that create clarity and bring the topic to life.

D. **Choosing words that deepen meaning:** The writer uses words to capture the reader's imagination and enhance the piece's meaning. There is a deliberate attempt to choose the best word over the first word that comes to mind.

A. **Applying strong verbs:** The writer uses the passive voice quite a bit and includes few action words to give the piece energy.

B. **Selecting striking words and phrases:** The writer provides little evidence that he or she has stretched for the best words or phrases. He or she may have attempted to use literary techniques, but they are clichés for the most part.

C. **Using specific and accurate words:** The writer presents specific and accurate words, except for those related to sophisticated and/or content-related topics. Technical or irrelevant jargon is off-putting to the reader. The words rarely capture the reader's imagination.

D. **Choosing words that deepen meaning:** The writer fills the piece with unoriginal language rather than language that results from careful revision. The words communicate the basic idea, but they are ordinary and uninspired.

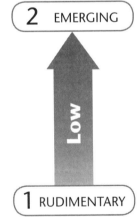

A. **Applying strong verbs:** The writer makes no attempt at selecting verbs with energy. The passive voice dominates the piece.

B. **Selecting striking words and phrases:** The writer uses words that are repetitive, vague, and/or unimaginative. Limited meaning comes through because the words are so lifeless.

C. **Using specific and accurate words:** The writer misuses words, making it difficult to understand what he or she is attempting to convey. Or he or she uses words that are so technical, inappropriate, or irrelevant that the average reader can hardly understand what he or she is saying.

D. **Choosing words that deepen meaning:** The writer uses many words and phrases that simply do not work. Little meaning comes through because the language is so imprecise and distracting.

Sentence Fluency

The way words and phrases flow through the piece—the auditory trait, because it's "read" with the ear as much as the eye

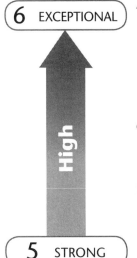

6 EXCEPTIONAL

A. **Crafting well-built sentences:** The writer carefully and creatively constructs sentences for maximum impact. Transition words such as *but*, *and*, and *so* are used successfully to join sentences and sentence parts.

B. **Varying sentence types:** The writer uses various types of sentences (simple, compound, and/or complex) to enhance the central theme or story line. The piece is made up of an effective mix of long, complex sentences and short, simple ones.

C. **Capturing smooth and rhythmic flow:** The writer thinks about how the sentences sound. He or she uses phrasing that is almost musical. If the piece were read aloud, it would be easy on the ear.

D. **Breaking the rules to create fluency:** The writer diverges from Standard English to create interest and impact. For example, he or she may use a sentence fragment, such as "All alone in the forest," or a single word, such as "Bam!" to accent a particular moment or action. He or she might begin with informal words such as *well*, *and*, or *but* to create a conversational tone, or he or she might break rules intentionally to make dialogue sound authentic.

5 STRONG

4 REFINING

A. **Crafting well-built sentences:** The writer offers simple sentences that are sound but not long or complex. He or she attempts to vary the beginnings and lengths of sentences.

B. **Varying sentence types:** The writer exhibits basic sentence sense and offers some sentence variety. He or she attempts to use different types of sentences but in doing so creates an uneven flow rather than a smooth, seamless one.

C. **Capturing smooth and rhythmic flow:** The writer has produced a text that is uneven. Many sentences read smoothly, whereas others are choppy or awkward.

D. **Breaking the rules to create fluency:** The writer includes fragments, but they seem more accidental than intentional. He or she uses informal words such as *well*, *and*, and *but* inappropriately to start sentences and pays little attention to making dialogue sound authentic.

3 DEVELOPING

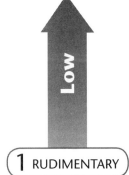

2 EMERGING

A. **Crafting well-built sentences:** The writer's sentences, even simple ones, are often flawed. Sentence beginnings are repetitive and uninspired.

B. **Varying sentence types:** The writer uses a single, repetitive sentence pattern throughout or connects sentence parts with an endless string of transition words such as *and*, *but*, *or*, and *because*, which distracts the reader.

C. **Capturing smooth and rhythmic flow:** The writer has created a text that is a challenge to read aloud since the sentences are incomplete, choppy, stilted, rambling, and/or awkward.

D. **Breaking the rules to create fluency:** The writer offers few or no simple, well-built sentences, making it impossible to determine whether he or she has done anything out of the ordinary. Global revision is necessary before sentences can be revised for stylistic and creative purposes.

1 RUDIMENTARY

page 5 of 7

Conventions

The mechanical correctness of the piece—correct use of conventions (spelling, capitalization, punctuation, paragraphing, and grammar and usage) guides the reader through the text easily

6 EXCEPTIONAL

5 STRONG

High

A. **Checking spelling:** The writer spells sight words, high-frequency words, and less familiar words correctly. When he or she spells less familiar words incorrectly, those words are phonetically correct. Overall, the piece reveals control in spelling.

B. **Punctuating effectively and paragraphing accurately:** The writer handles basic punctuation skillfully. He or she understands how to use periods, commas, question marks, and exclamation points to enhance clarity and meaning. Paragraphs are indented in the right places. The piece is ready for a general audience.

C. **Capitalizing correctly:** The writer uses capital letters consistently and accurately. A deep understanding of how to capitalize dialogue, abbreviations, proper names, and titles is evident.

D. **Applying grammar and usage:** The writer forms grammatically correct phrases and sentences. He or she shows care in applying the rules of Standard English. The writer may break from those rules for stylistic reasons but otherwise abides by them.

4 REFINING

3 DEVELOPING

Middle

A. **Checking spelling:** The writer incorrectly spells a few high-frequency words and many unfamiliar words and/or sophisticated words.

B. **Punctuating effectively and paragraphing accurately:** The writer handles basic punctuation marks (such as end marks on sentences and commas in a series) well. However, he or she might have trouble with more complex punctuation marks (such as quotation marks, parentheses, and dashes) and with paragraphing, especially on longer pieces.

C. **Capitalizing correctly:** The writer capitalizes the first word in sentences and most common proper nouns. However, his or her use of more complex capitalization is spotty when it comes to dialogue, abbreviations, and proper names ("aunt Maria" instead of "Aunt Maria" or "my aunt," for instance).

D. **Applying grammar and usage:** The writer has made grammar and usage mistakes throughout the piece, but they do not interfere with the reader's ability to understand the message. Issues related to agreement, tense, and word usage appear here and there but can be easily corrected.

2 EMERGING

1 RUDIMENTARY

Low

A. **Checking spelling:** The writer has misspelled many words, even simple ones, which causes the reader to focus on conventions rather than on the central theme or story line.

B. **Punctuating effectively and paragraphing accurately:** The writer has neglected to use punctuation, used punctuation incorrectly, and/or forgotten to indent paragraphs, making it difficult for the reader to find meaning.

C. **Capitalizing correctly:** The writer uses capitals inconsistently, even in common places such as the first word in the sentence. He or she uses capitals correctly in some places but has no consistent control over them.

D. **Applying grammar and usage:** The writer makes frequent mistakes in grammar and usage, making it difficult to read and understand the piece. Issues related to agreement, tense, and word usage abound.

page 6 of 7

Presentation

The physical appearance of the piece—a visually appealing text provides a welcome mat and invites the reader in

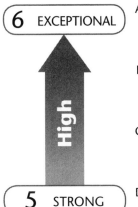

6 EXCEPTIONAL

High

5 STRONG

A. **Applying handwriting skills:** The writer uses handwriting that is clear and legible. Whether he or she prints or uses cursive, letters are uniform and slant evenly throughout the piece. Spacing between words is consistent.

B. **Using word processing effectively:** The writer uses a font style and size that are easy to read and are a good match for the piece's purpose. If he or she uses color, it enhances the piece's readability.

C. **Making good use of white space:** The writer frames the text with appropriately sized margins. Artful spacing between letters, words, and lines makes reading a breeze. There are no cross-outs, smudges, or tears on the paper.

D. **Refining text features:** The writer effectively places text features such as headings, page numbers, titles, and bullets on the page and aligns them clearly with the text they support.

4 REFINING

Middle

3 DEVELOPING

A. **Applying handwriting skills:** The writer has readable handwriting, but his or her inconsistent letter slanting, spacing, and formation distract from the central theme or story line.

B. **Using word processing effectively:** The writer uses an easy-to-read font but formats it in a way that makes the piece cluttered and distracting. His or her choice of font style and size may not match the writing's purpose. He or she may use color with varying degrees of success.

C. **Making good use of white space:** The writer creates margins but they are inconsistent or ineffective as a frame for the piece. Spacing between letters, words, and lines makes reading difficult at times. An occasional cross-out or smudge blemishes the piece.

D. **Refining text features:** The writer includes complex text features such as charts, graphs, maps, and tables, but not clearly or consistently. However, he or she does a good job with less complex features such as the size and placement of the title, bullets, sidebars, subheadings, illustrations, and page numbers.

2 EMERGING

Low

1 RUDIMENTARY

A. **Applying handwriting skills:** The writer forms letters and uses space in a way that makes the piece virtually illegible. The handwriting is a visual barrier.

B. **Using word processing effectively:** The writer creates a dizzying display of different font styles and sizes, making the piece virtually unreadable. The misuse of color also detracts.

C. **Making good use of white space:** The writer formats margins inconsistently and uses white space ineffectively, making the piece hard to read. Space between letters, words, and lines is nonexistent, or there is so much space it's distracting.

D. **Refining text features:** The writer does not include features or includes features that are confusing or indecipherable rather than useful to the reader. The paper is seriously marred with cross-outs, smudges, or tears.

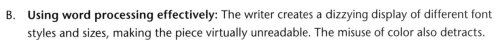

Source: Reprinted with permission of Scholastic, Inc.

page 7 of 7

Student-Friendly Scoring Guide for Beginning Writers

Ideas

How you explore the main point or story of your writing

I've Got It!

- I know A LOT about my topic.

- My writing is bursting with fascinating details.

- I've picked a topic that's focused enough to handle.

STRONG

On My Way

- I know enough about my topic to get started.

- Some of my details are too general.

- My topic might be a little too big.

DEVELOPING

Just Beginning

- I haven't figured out what to say.

- My details aren't clear.

- I'm still thinking about and looking for a topic.

BEGINNING

page 1 of 7

Organization

How you connect the ideas from beginning to end

I've Got It!

- I have a bold beginning, mighty middle, and excellent ending.

- All of my details are in the right places.

- The order of my ideas really works.

STRONG

On My Way

- My beginning, middle, and ending are off to a good start.

- Most of my details fit.

- The order of my ideas makes sense.

DEVELOPING

Just Beginning

- My writing doesn't have a clear beginning, middle, or ending.

- My details are jumbled and confusing.

- I have stuff on paper, but it's not in order.

BEGINNING

page 2 of 7

Voice

How you express ideas with energy and pizzazz

STRONG

I've Got It!

- My writing sounds like me.

- The reader will know I care about my topic.

- I have the right amount of energy in this piece.

DEVELOPING

On My Way

- My writing is safe. The reader only gets a glimpse of me.

- I care a little about this topic.

- My energy is uneven in this piece.

BEGINNING

Just Beginning

- I forgot to say what I think and feel about my topic.

- I really don't care at all about the topic.

- I'm bored, and it shows.

Word Choice

How you use words and phrases to create meaning

STRONG

I've Got It!

- I've picked exactly the right words.
- My words are colorful, fresh, and snappy.
- The words help my reader see my ideas.

DEVELOPING

On My Way

- Some of my words work well, but others don't.
- I've used too many ordinary words.
- My words paint a general picture of the idea.

BEGINNING

Just Beginning

- I'm not sure how to use words well.
- I've left out key words.
- Many of my words are the same or don't make sense.

page 4 of 7

Sentence Fluency

How you construct sentences so they sound smooth

STRONG

I've Got It!

- My sentences are well-built and easy to read aloud.

- The way my sentences begin makes my writing interesting.

- I've varied my sentence lengths.

DEVELOPING

On My Way

- I've got sentences! Some of them are hard to read aloud, though.

- A couple of my sentences begin in different ways.

- I might join short sentences or cut long ones in two.

BEGINNING

Just Beginning

- I am having trouble making a sentence.

- My beginnings all sound the same.

- I haven't varied my sentence lengths at all.

page 5 of 7

Conventions

How you edit text to make it readable

I've Got It!

- My spelling is magnificent.

- All my capitals are in the right place.

- I used punctuation correctly.

- I've used correct grammar and added paragraphs where needed.

- I've done a great job proofreading.

STRONG

On My Way

- Only simple words are spelled correctly.

- I've used capitals in easy spots.

- I've used correct punctuation in some places but not in others.

- I proofread quickly and missed things.

DEVELOPING

Just Beginning

- My spelling makes it hard to read my words.

- I haven't followed capitalization rules.

- I haven't used punctuation well at all.

- I forgot to proofread.

BEGINNING

Presentation

How you create visual appeal

STRONG

I've Got It!

- My paper is neat—no smudges or cross-outs.
- My letters are neatly formed.
- My margins frame my writing.

DEVELOPING

On My Way

- My paper can be read, but it's not easy.
- Some of my letters are neatly formed, but some are not.
- My margins work in some places, but not in others.

BEGINNING

Just Beginning

- My paper is very hard to read.
- My letters are not neatly formed at all.
- I forgot to use margins.

Reprinted with permission of Scholastic, Inc.

Student-Friendly Scoring Guide for Established Writers A

Ideas

How you explore the main point or story of your writing

I've Got It!

6

- I picked a topic and stuck with it.
- My topic is small enough to handle.
- I know a lot about this topic.
- My topic is bursting with fascinating details.

5

On My Way

4

- I've wandered off my main topic in a few places.
- My topic might be a little too big to handle.
- I know enough about my topic to get started.
- Some of my details are too general.

3

Just Beginning

2

- I have included several ideas that might make a good topic.
- No one idea stands out as most important.
- I'm still looking for a topic that will work well.
- My details are fuzzy or not clear.

1

Organization

How you connect the ideas from beginning to end

I've Got It!

- I included a bold beginning.
- I've shown how the ideas connect.
- My ideas are in an order that really works.
- My ending leaves you with something to think about.

On My Way

- There is a beginning, but it's not particularly special.
- Most of my details fit logically; I could move or get rid of others.
- Sections of my writing flow logically, but other parts seem out of place.
- My ending is not original, but it does clearly show where the piece stops.

Just Beginning

- I forgot to write a clear introduction to this piece.
- I have the right stuff to work with, but it's not in order.
- The order of my details is jumbled and confusing.
- Oops! I forgot to end my piece with a wrap-up.

page 2 of 7

Voice

How you express your ideas with energy and pizzazz

I've Got It!

6

5

- I used a distinctive tone that works with the topic.
- I was clear about why I was writing, so my voice is believable.
- The audience will connect with what I wrote.
- I tried some new ways of expressing myself to add interest.

On My Way

4

3

- I played it safe. You only get a glimpse of me in this piece.
- I wasn't always clear about my purpose, so my voice fades in and out.
- I'm only mildly interested in this topic.
- I didn't try to express myself in new ways.

Just Beginning

2

1

- I didn't share anything about what I think and feel in this piece.
- I'm not sure what or why I'm writing.
- This topic is not interesting to me at all.
- I'm bored, and it shows.

Word Choice

How you use words and phrases to create meaning

6

5

I've Got It!

- I used strong verbs to add energy.
- My words are specific and are colorful, fresh, and snappy.
- My words help my reader see my ideas.
- My words are accurate and used correctly.

4

3

On My Way

- Only one or two verbs stand out in this piece.
- I've used many ordinary words; there's no sparkle.
- My words give the reader the most general picture of the idea.
- I've misused some words or overused others.

2

1

Just Beginning

- I haven't used any verbs that convey energy.
- I've left out key words.
- Many of my words are repetitive or just wrong.
- I'm confused about how to use words as I write.

Sentence Fluency

How you construct sentences so they sound smooth

I've Got It!

6

- My sentences are well built and have varied beginnings.

- I've tried to write using interjections or fragments to create variety.

5

- My sentences read smoothly.

- I've varied the length and structure of my sentences.

On My Way

- My sentences are working pretty well.

4

- I've tried a couple of ways to begin my sentences differently but could do more.

3

- When I read my piece aloud, there are a few places that need smoothing.

- I might put some sentences together, or I could cut a few in two.

Just Beginning

2

- My sentences aren't working well.

- The beginnings of my sentences sound the same.

1

- I'm having trouble reading my piece aloud.

- I've used words like *and* or *but* too many times.

page 5 of 7

Conventions

How you edit text to make it readable

I've Got It!

- My spelling is magnificent.

- I put capital letters in all the right places.

- I used punctuation correctly to make my writing easy to read.

- I used correct grammar and indented paragraphs where necessary.

On My Way

- Only my simpler words are spelled correctly.

- I used capital letters in easy spots.

- I have correct punctuation in some places but not in others.

- There are a few places where the grammar isn't quite right, and I've forgotten to indicate paragraphs except at the beginning.

Just Beginning

- My words are hard to read and understand because of the spelling.

- I've not followed the rules for capitalization.

- My punctuation is missing or in the wrong places.

- The grammar needs a lot of work. I forgot about using paragraphs.

Presentation

How you create visual appeal

I've Got It!

- I've used my very best handwriting.
- My font choices are very readable.
- The margins on my paper are even and frame the writing.
- I've used a heading, numbered pages, and a bulleted list or fancy capital.

On My Way

- My handwriting is readable, but it's not my best.
- I picked one main font but then added too many fancy fonts.
- I started out with even margins, but they didn't end up that way.
- I put my name and date on my paper, but I didn't try anything else.

Just Beginning

- Yikes! I'm having a hard time reading my own handwriting.
- My fonts are distracting.
- I didn't use margins, and my writing doesn't have white space.
- I forgot all about adding my name, the date, page numbers, and more.

Student-Friendly Scoring Guide for Established Writers B

Ideas

The piece's content—its central message and the details that support that message

6 EXPERT

High

5 WELL DONE

My topic is well developed and focused. My piece contains specific, interesting, and accurate details and new thinking about this topic.

- I have a clear central theme or a simple, original story line.

- I've narrowed my theme or story line to create a focused piece that is a pleasure to read.

- I've included original information to support my main idea.

- I've included specific, interesting, and accurate details that will create pictures in the reader's mind.

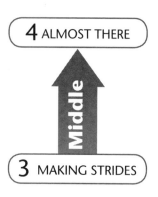

4 ALMOST THERE

Middle

3 MAKING STRIDES

My piece includes many general observations about the topic but lacks focus and clear, accurate details. I need to elaborate.

- I've stayed on the topic, but my theme or story line is too broad.

- I haven't dug into the topic in a logical, focused way.

- My unique perspective on this topic is not coming through as clearly as it could.

- The reader may have questions after reading this piece, because my details leave some questions unanswered.

2 ON MY WAY

Low

1 GETTING STARTED

I'm still thinking about the theme or story line for this piece. So far, I've only explored possibilities.

- I've jotted down some ideas for topics, but it's a hodgepodge.

- Nothing in particular stands out as important in my piece.

- I have not written much. I may have only restated the assignment.

- My details are thin and need to be checked for accuracy.

page 1 of 7

Organization

The internal structure of a piece—the thread of logic and the pattern of meaning

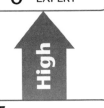

My details unfold in a logical order. The structure makes reading my piece a breeze.

- My beginning grabs the reader's attention.

- I've used sequence and transition words to guide the reader.

- All of my details fit together logically and move along smoothly.

- My ending gives the reader a sense of closure and something to think about.

My piece's organization is pretty basic and predictable. I have the three essential ingredients—a beginning, middle, and end—but that's about it.

- My beginning is clear but unoriginal. I've used a technique that writers use all too often.

- I've used simple sequence and transition words that stand out too much.

- Details need to be added or moved around to create a more logical flow of ideas.

- My ending needs work; it's pretty canned.

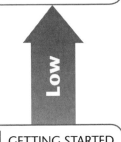

My piece doesn't make much sense, because I haven't figured out a way to organize it. The details are jumbled together at this point.

- My beginning doesn't indicate where I'm going or why I'm going there.

- I have not grouped ideas or connected them using sequence and transition words.

- With no sense of order, it will be a challenge for the reader to sort out how the details relate.

- I haven't figured out how to end this piece.

Voice

The tone and tenor of the piece—the personal stamp of the writer, which is achieved through a strong understanding of purpose and audience

I've come up with my own take on the topic. I had my audience and purpose clearly in mind as I wrote, and I presented my ideas in an original way.

- My piece is expressive, which shows how much I care about my topic.

- The purpose for this piece is clear, and I've used a tone that suits that purpose.

- There is no doubt in my mind that the reader will understand how I think and feel about my topic.

- I've expressed myself in some new, original ways.

My feelings about the topic come across as uninspired and predictable. The piece is not all that expressive, nor does it reveal a commitment to the topic.

- My authentic voice comes through but only in a few places.

- My purpose for writing this piece is unclear to me, so the tone feels off.

- I've made little effort to connect with the reader; I'm playing it safe.

- This piece sounds like lots of others on this topic. It's not very original.

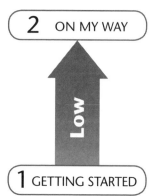

I haven't thought at all about my purpose or audience for the piece, and therefore my voice falls flat. I'm pretty indifferent to the topic, and it shows.

- I've put no energy into this piece.

- My purpose for writing this piece is a mystery to me, so I'm casting about aimlessly.

- Since my topic isn't interesting to me, chances are my piece won't be interesting to the reader. I haven't thought about my audience.

- I have taken no risks. There is no evidence that I find this topic interesting or care about it at all.

page 3 of 7

Word Choice

The specific vocabulary you use to convey meaning and enlighten the reader

The words and phrases I've selected are accurate, specific, and natural sounding. My piece conveys precisely what I want to say because of my powerful vocabulary.

- My piece contains strong verbs that bring it alive.

- I stretched by using the perfect words and phrases to convey my ideas.

- I've used content words and phrases with accuracy and precision.

- I've picked the best words and phrases, not just the first ones that came to mind.

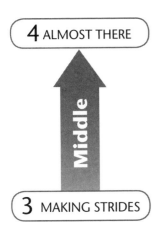

My words and phrases make sense but aren't very accurate, specific, or natural sounding. The reader won't have trouble understanding them. However, he or she may find them uninspiring.

- I've used passive voice. I should rethink passages that contain passive voice and add action words.

- I haven't come up with extraordinary ways to say ordinary things.

- My content words and phrases are accurate but general. I might have overused jargon. I need to choose words that are more precise.

- I need to revise this piece by replacing its weak words and phrases with strong ones.

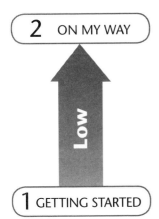

My words and phrases are so unclear the reader may wind up more confused than entertained, informed, or persuaded. I need to expand my vocabulary to improve this piece.

- My verbs are not strong. Passive voice permeates this piece.

- I've used bland words and phrases throughout—or the same words and phrases over and over.

- My content words are neither specific nor accurate enough to make the meaning clear.

- My words and phrases are not working; they distract the reader rather than guide him or her.

Sentence Fluency

The way the words and phrases flow through the piece—the auditory trait, because it's "read" with the ear as much as the eye

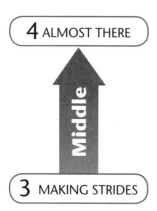

6 EXPERT

5 WELL DONE

My piece is strong because I've written a variety of well-built sentences. I've woven those sentences together to create a smooth-sounding piece.

- I've constructed and connected my sentences for maximum impact.

- I've varied my sentence lengths and types—short and long, simple and complex.

- When I read my piece aloud, it is pleasing to my ear.

- I've broken grammar rules intentionally at points to create impact and interest.

4 ALMOST THERE

3 MAKING STRIDES

Although my sentences lack variety or creativity, most of them are grammatically correct. Some of them are smooth, while others are choppy and awkward.

- I've written solid shorter sentences. Now I need to try some longer ones.

- I've created different kinds of sentences, but the result is uneven.

- When I read my piece aloud, I stumble in a few places.

- Any sentences that break grammar rules are accidental and don't work well.

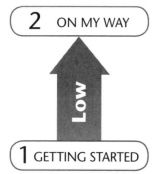

2 ON MY WAY

1 GETTING STARTED

My sentences are choppy, incomplete, or rambling. I need to revise my piece extensively to make it more readable.

- Many of my sentences don't work because they're poorly constructed.

- I've used the same sentence lengths and types over and over again.

- When I read my piece aloud, I stumble in many places.

- If I've broken grammar rules, it's not for stylistic reasons—it's because I may not understand those rules.

Conventions

The mechanical correctness of the piece—correct use of conventions (spelling, capitalization, punctuation, paragraphing, and grammar and usage), which guides the reader through the text easily

My piece proves I can use a range of conventions with skill and creativity. It is ready for its intended audience.

- My spelling is strong. I've spelled all or nearly all the words accurately.

- I've used punctuation creatively and correctly and have begun new paragraphs in the right places.

- I've used capital letters correctly throughout my piece, even in tricky places.

- I've taken care to apply Standard English grammar and usage.

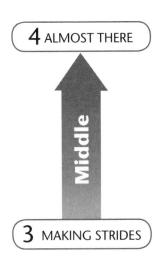

My writing still needs editing to correct problems in one or more conventions. I've stuck to the basics and haven't tried challenging conventions.

- I've misspelled words that I use all the time, as well as complex words that I don't use as often.

- My punctuation is basically strong, but I should review it one more time. I indented some of the paragraphs but not all of them.

- I've correctly used capital letters in obvious places (such as the word *I*) but not in others.

- Even though my grammar and usage are not 100 percent correct, my audience should be able to read my piece.

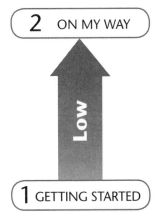

The problems I'm having with conventions make this piece challenging to read, even for me! I've got lots of work to do before it's ready for its intended audience.

- Extensive spelling errors make my piece difficult to read and understand.

- I haven't punctuated or paragraphed the piece well, which makes it difficult for the reader to understand or enjoy my writing.

- My use of capital letters is so inconsistent, it's distracting.

- I need to clean up the piece considerably in terms of grammar and usage.

page 6 of 7

Presentation

The physical appearance of the piece, which—when visually appealing—provides a welcome mat and invites the reader in

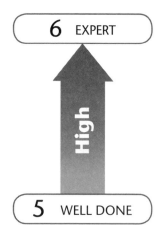

My piece's appearance makes it easy to read and enjoy. I've taken care to ensure that it is pleasing to my reader's eye.

- I've written clearly and legibly. My letters and words and the spaces between them are uniform.

- My choice of font style, size, and/or color makes my piece a breeze to read.

- My margins frame the text nicely. There are no tears, smudges, or cross-outs.

- Text features such as bulleted lists, charts, pictures, and headers are working well.

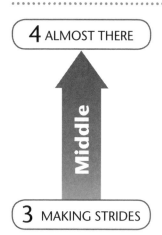

My piece still looks like a draft. Many visual elements should be cleaned up and handled with more care.

- My handwriting is readable, but my letters and words and the spaces between them should be treated more consistently.

- My choice of font style, size, and/or color seems off—inappropriate for my intended audience.

- My margins are uneven. There are some tears, smudges, or cross-outs.

- I've handled simple text features well but am struggling with the more complex ones.

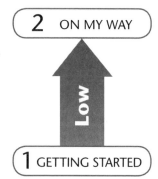

My piece is almost unreadable because of its appearance. It's not ready for anyone but me to read.

- My handwriting is so hard to read it creates a visual barrier.

- The font styles, sizes, and/or colors I've chosen are dizzying. They're not working.

- My margins are uneven or nonexistent, making the piece difficult to read.

- I haven't used text features well, even simple ones.

Source: Reprinted with permission of Scholastic, Inc.

What Principals Need to Know About Teaching and Learning Writing © 2014 Solution Tree Press • solution-tree.com
Visit **go.solution-tree.com/leadership** to download this page.

Teacher-Friendly Scoring Guide for Narrative Writing

Purpose: To tell a story

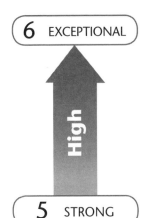

6 EXCEPTIONAL

High

5 STRONG

- The writer starts with a lead that sets up the story and draws the reader in.
- The writer includes fresh, believable characters that grow and learn.
- The writer offers a rich setting that is easy to visualize.
- The writer includes events that are logically sequenced and move the story forward. Time and place work in harmony.
- The writer tells a completely new story or puts an original twist on a familiar story. The plot is well developed. There is a compelling conflict or problem that is eventually solved.
- The writer uses literary techniques, such as foreshadowing, symbolism, and figurative language, well.
- The writer leaves the reader feeling intrigued, surprised, or entertained.
- The writer solves the compelling conflict or problem thoughtfully and credibly.

4 REFINING

Middle

3 DEVELOPING

- The writer starts with a lead that sets the scene but is predictable or unoriginal.
- The writer includes characters that are a bit too familiar. His or her thinking or understanding hardly changes as the story progresses.
- The writer offers a predictable setting that is somewhat easy to visualize.
- The writer devotes the same level of importance to events. Significant events mingle with trivial ones and sometimes stray from the story line.
- The writer tells a nearly complete story that may not contain new or original thinking. The writer presents minor conflicts and problems that distract from major ones.
- The writer uses literary techniques but not all that effectively.
- The writer engages the reader at some points but not at others.
- The writer ends with a sense of resolution, but the reader may feel unsatisfied and/or perplexed.

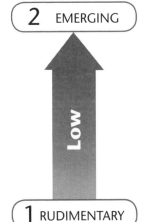

2 EMERGING

Low

1 RUDIMENTARY

- The writer starts with a perfunctory lead: "I'm going to tell you about the time. . . ."
- The writer includes characters that don't feel real. They feel more like stereotypes or cardboard cutouts.
- The writer offers a setting that is almost impossible to visualize.
- The writer includes simple, unrelated events that don't add up to anything much.
- The writer jumps around illogically. There is no clear conflict or problem to be solved.
- The writer does not use literary techniques or uses them imprecisely or with no clear purpose.
- The writer leaves the reader frustrated or disappointed. He or she did not think through the story before committing it to paper.
- The writer finishes with no clear ending or, at most, a halfhearted ending, leaving the reader wondering why he or she bothered.

Source: Reprinted with permission of Scholastic, Inc.

Teacher-Friendly Scoring Guide for Informational/Explanatory Writing

Purpose: To convey complex information clearly and accurately

6 EXCEPTIONAL

High

5 STRONG

- The writer delves into what really matters about the topic.
- The writer offers an insider's perspective.
- The writer provides unexpected or surprising details.
- The writer is focused, coherent, and well organized.
- The writer invites the reader to analyze and synthesize details in order to draw his or her own conclusions.
- The writer includes many fascinating, original, accurate facts that are, when appropriate, linked to primary sources.
- The writer tells anecdotes that bring the topic to life.
- The writer anticipates and answers the reader's questions.
- The writer stays on point and uses a compelling voice until the end.

4 REFINING

Middle

3 DEVELOPING

- The writer provides an overview of the topic and only a few key facts.
- The writer offers the perspective of an outsider looking in.
- The writer lacks fresh thinking or surprises. He or she relies too heavily on common knowledge and provides mostly mundane, predictable details about the topic.
- The writer is relatively focused, coherent, and organized and generally stays on topic.
- The writer provides focused descriptions but fuzzy ones, too. The writer doesn't consistently connect the dots.
- The writer includes facts that are somewhat suspicious and not linked to primary sources.
- The writer tells few, if any, anecdotes to bring the topic to life.
- The writer does not anticipate the reader's questions.
- The writer speaks in a spotty voice—commanding one moment, cautious the next.

2 EMERGING

Low

1 RUDIMENTARY

- The writer misses the main point completely. His or her purpose is not clear.
- The writer offers a complete outsider's perspective.
- The writer includes details that are completely unrelated to the main topic.
- The writer is unfocused, incoherent, and poorly organized.
- The writer makes sweeping statements. Nothing new is shared.
- The writer provides no fascinating, original facts. Any facts the piece does contain seem inaccurate or unsupported.
- The writer tells no anecdotes to bring the topic to life.
- The writer does not anticipate the reader's questions. In fact, the piece contains no evidence that he or she has thought about audience at all. The piece is difficult to read from beginning to end.

Source: Reprinted with permission of Scholastic, Inc.

Teacher-Friendly Scoring Guide for Argument Writing

Purpose: To use valid reasoning and relevant and sufficient evidence to support claims on substantive topics

6 EXCEPTIONAL

High

5 STRONG

- The writer influences the reader with sound reasoning and a compelling argument.
- The writer offers opinions that are well supported by facts and personal experiences. Differences between facts and personal experiences are clear.
- The writer takes a position that is defensible and logical.
- The writer exposes the weaknesses of other positions.
- The writer avoids generalities and exaggerations.
- The writer includes a lot of sound reasoning and judgment.
- The writer uses only the best evidence to make the strongest statement possible.
- The writer connects to a larger "truth."

4 REFINING

Middle

3 DEVELOPING

- The writer raises questions for the reader but may fail to persuade him or her because the thinking is superficial.
- The writer mixes opinions, facts, and personal experiences. The piece relies on emotion more than truth. Data may be present, but they are not used effectively.
- The writer gives an argument that starts out strong but fades. He or she offers few insights.
- The writer attempts to expose flaws in other positions, with mixed results.
- The writer features concrete information but also generalities or exaggerations.
- The writer includes some sound reasoning and judgment.
- The writer puts forth some evidence that hits the mark, and some that doesn't.
- The writer waffles. Some statements are plausible and others are far-fetched, leaving the reader unconvinced.
- The writer does not influence the reader. His or her thinking is vulnerable to attack.

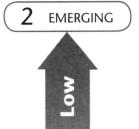

2 EMERGING

Low

1 RUDIMENTARY

- The writer offers opinions that are not supported by facts or personal experiences.
- The writer takes a position that is not clear or credible. The argument is illogical or implausible.
- The writer ignores the opposing side of the argument.
- The writer provides only generalities and exaggerations but no hard facts that could sway the reader.
- The writer uses little or no sound reasoning and judgment.
- The writer ignores the evidence necessary for the reader to take a stand.
- The writer does not question or probe. The piece misses the target.

Source: Reprinted with permission of Scholastic, Inc.

Grading Chart

Grade	Points	Number of Criteria						
		7	6	5	4	3	2	1
	1							60.00%
	2						60.00%	68.00%
	3					60.00%	64.00%	76.00%
	4				60.00%	62.67%	68.00%	84.00%
	5			60.00%	62.00%	65.33%	72.00%	92.00%
	6		60.00%	61.60%	64.00%	68.00%	76.00%	100.00%
F	7	60.00%	61.33%	63.20%	66.00%	70.67%	80.00%	
	8	61.14%	62.67%	64.80%	68.00%	73.33%	84.00%	
	9	62.29%	64.00%	66.40%	70.00%	76.00%	88.00%	
	10	63.43%	65.33%	68.00%	72.00%	78.67%	92.00%	
	11	64.57%	66.67%	69.60%	74.00%	81.33%	96.00%	
	12	65.71%	68.00%	71.20%	76.00%	84.00%	100.00%	
	13	66.86%	69.33%	72.80%	78.00%	86.67%		
D	14	68.00%	70.67%	74.40%	80.00%	89.33%		
	15	69.14%	72.00%	76.00%	82.00%	92.00%		
	16	70.29%	73.33%	77.60%	84.00%	94.67%		
	17	71.43%	74.67%	79.20%	86.00%	97.33%		
	18	72.57%	76.00%	80.80%	88.00%	100.00%		
	19	73.71%	77.33%	82.40%	90.00%			
	20	74.86%	78.67%	84.00%	92.00%			
C	21	76.00%	80.00%	85.60%	94.00%			
	22	77.14%	81.33%	87.20%	96.00%			
	23	78.29%	82.67%	88.80%	98.00%			
	24	79.43%	84.00%	90.40%	100.00%			
	25	80.57%	85.33%	92.00%				
	26	81.71%	86.67%	93.60%				
	27	82.86%	88.00%	95.20%				
B	28	84.00%	89.33%	96.80%				
	29	85.14%	90.67%	98.40%				
	30	86.29%	92.00%	100.00%				
	31	87.43%	93.33%					
	32	88.57%	94.67%					
	33	89.71%	96.00%					
	34	90.86%	97.33%					
A	35	92.00%	98.67%					
	36	93.14%	100.00%					
	37	94.29%						
	38	95.43%						
	39	96.57%						
	40	97.71%						
	41	98.86%						
A+	42	100.00%						

Source: Reprinted with permission of Scholastic, Inc.

FIVE

ASSESSING THE TEACHING OF WRITING

In a school that cherishes writing, writing is not a subject area. It is what students do throughout the day, because it is valued and purposeful. In a school that values writing, students get feedback during the process, not just at the end. They use the language of the traits to dive into the writing looking for what works and what needs to be worked on further. They get this feedback from the teacher and each other and discover that assessment is one of the best tools in their writing toolbox. Students learn that writing improves over time and that just getting it done is not the goal.

—John Z. Nittolo, Superintendent/Principal, Green Hills
School, Greendell, New Jersey

Whether writing instruction has been at the forefront of your school's improvement plan for the last several years or you are just beginning to focus on it, this chapter will help you figure out what to do next. By using the Writing Teacher's Self-Assessment (page 87) in this chapter, teachers will have a chance to figure out where they are doing a great job teaching writing and where they could use more support. As they share their insights from this assessment, you can help individuals and groups of teachers focus on how to maximize the benefits of using the 4Ws. As Susan Brookhart and Connie Moss (2013) write, the knowledge from formative assessments "opens the door for the principal to identify areas in which teachers are already successful and areas in which they may need more assistance. Armed with that information, principals are able to have deeper and richer conversations with teachers about their practice" (p. 13).

Using the Teacher's Self-Assessment

At a staff meeting, ask teachers to spend about ten minutes completing the Writing Teacher's Self-Assessment (page 87). Ask them to be completely honest and to circle the descriptors in each category that best match how they feel about their writing instruction practices. This should be a nonthreatening activity, so if you do it first, it will set that tone. Show them how you've filled out your own self-evaluation and how you are all over the place in terms of the categories. Explain that you would like to use their assessments to set goals for the school year, and ask them to highlight or star at least two categories they'd like to be the focus of professional development, either for the whole staff or for themselves as individuals. You'll note that the headings in the Writing Teacher's Self-Assessment—Writing Neophyte, Writing Dabbler, Writing Apprentice, Writing Go-Getter, and Writing Guru—are intended to make this a user-friendly task.

After teachers complete the task, ask them to share with a colleague where they feel the most important professional development is needed. Encourage them to discuss insights and observations about how they scored themselves, but don't insist. Some teachers may not be comfortable sharing, and that's okay. Explain that the intent is for teachers to begin talking about what is going well and what they need help to improve, so as a team, you can begin to address concerns and support ideas for taking writing at the school to a whole new level. By sharing your own assessment, you let them know that it's okay not to be in the ideal place in every category as you begin this work together. Let them know they are shooting for Writing Go-Getter, and some of them will even reach Writing Guru, but it will take time to hit these higher levels of writing instruction with ease.

If teachers feel their responses will be used against them in any way, they will not be honest. And you want honest answers so you can set the stage for growth and change. Bottom line: it's perfectly fine that every teacher isn't where he or she wants to be on this first assessment. It's not perfectly fine for any of them to be in this same place by the end of the year, however. The emphasis in this activity should be to gather information and focus on writing instruction—with a light touch. Assessment doesn't always have to be intimidating. Think of this document as a place to begin your work together as a staff and see where it takes you.

Setting Goals and Providing Support

Teachers have various backgrounds and attitudes regarding writing instruction. Some come from traditional backgrounds in which grammar skills and practice were routinely handled as worksheets. Others have embraced writing workshops and believe that writing instruction should be highly individual. In most cases, the majority of the staff will fall somewhere in between the highly structured and unstructured approaches.

At the goal-setting conference, start with the highlighted or starred categories and where the teacher feels he or she is on the scale, and then compare that to the teacher's impression of where writing instruction for the whole school might score. Teachers may feel that they are ahead of others or behind—regardless, it's insightful to see what each teacher thinks about writing instruction and where each is now compared to where he or she would like to be.

Make sure teachers understand that marking themselves in a beginning place for any category is not a problem. If a teacher marks him- or herself as "writing neophyte" in writing assessment and writing modes, for instance, let that teacher know you appreciate the honesty and you plan to give your support as he or she tackles these areas for improvement. The purpose is to find out where teachers want to grow and improve, not just to gloss over the hard parts of teaching writing out of fear of looking like they don't know everything. No one knows everything. Trust me on that! If there is anything about teaching writing I've learned in the last forty years, it's that it's hard, it's complex, and it's never ending—but when you begin to see that what you are doing makes a difference, it's ultimately satisfying.

Try to keep the conversations concrete and constructive, urging teachers to tell you which of the following forms of support would be useful to them:

- Professional development on a specific writing-related topic

- Observing another teacher teaching writing

- Aligning grade-level curriculum in writing to ensure maximum content in writing instruction across the grades

- Working with a colleague to integrate new resources into instructional units

- Finding books and resource materials that provide inspiration and motivation

- Taking online classes or classes from a local college or university

- Team teaching with a literacy coach on a lesson or two

- Learning how to apply technology to the writing classroom

- Visiting another school that has experienced success with writing

- Developing writing lessons and activities with grade-level teammates

- Using the school website to publish student writing

- Assessing writing with colleagues to determine what is working well and what is needed next to improve writing instruction

Develop a plan for each teacher that clearly specifies what skills the teacher agrees to improve and how you can facilitate that learning. One form for this mutual agreement might look like the reproducible Teaching Writing Agreement on page 90.

Depending on the course of action you take with each teacher, use the following checklists (pages 91–99 and at **go.solution-tree.com/leadership**) for visits to classrooms:

- Where Writers Thrive Checklist

- What Teachers and Students Need Checklist

- How Writing Teachers Teach Checklist

- How Writers Learn From Others Checklist

- How Writers Get Energized Checklist

- Writing Process Checklist

- The Traits of Writing Checklist

- Writing Modes and Purposes Checklist

- Progress and Grades Checklist

You may want to use more than one of these forms and share your observations with the teacher after your classroom visits.

The next and final chapter discusses how, apart from higher test scores, you can know your school's writing program is working well and that teachers and students are thriving in a positive, productive learning environment that supports them both.

Writing Teacher's Self-Assessment

	Writing Neophyte	Writing Dabbler	Writing Apprentice	Writing Go-Getter	Writing Guru
How I Approach Writing	My students spend about forty-five minutes per week on writing skills, using worksheets or the grammar handbook. We don't create any pieces of writing outside of the short pieces from our textbook.	I pretty much just assign any writing we do. I have no idea how to teach it other than how it was taught to me. We spend about eighty minutes in writing activities each week.	I've thought about doing things differently, but I need help to know what to do next. I'd like to collaborate more. I plan about thirty minutes a day for writing, but it doesn't always happen.	Our school has organized into learning teams, and we collaborate on writing as well as other areas. I'm trying new ways of teaching writing and looking for more ideas to try, too. We spend at least forty minutes a day learning about and doing writing.	I've invited other teachers to observe during writing time and then set up time to talk afterward. My students write about everything all the time for long and short periods at the drop of a hat! My students rock at writing! I share what I'm learning with others in the school as we work together to improve writing instruction.
How Writers Work in My Classroom	My students write the same thing at the same time, regardless of their skill level. I prefer the classroom to be quiet when they work.	I'm struggling with how to help writers who aren't as skilled as others. I let my students talk to each other as they work, but it's pretty noisy and distracting.	I'm experimenting with writing groups, but I'm having trouble managing it all. It feels like the right direction, however. My students are louder than necessary as they work.	I've taught my students how to work independently when I'm working with others. So far, so good. They talk quietly but not always about writing and wait for me to come and help with their questions.	In my classroom, students have learned that writing is a way to think aloud on paper, so they've also learned to use each other, not just me, as a resource. There's a quiet but busy hum during writing time.
What I Use to Teach Writing	All of our writing lessons and activities come from a text or are done on worksheets.	I've pulled together teaching ideas from several sources to supplement the textbook and the curriculum.	I'm trying out lessons specific to the traits and modes, and my resources have expanded beyond the text and worksheets. I rarely use worksheets anymore.	I've found some print and nonprint materials to teach writing using the traits and modes. I'm looking for more all the time. My students practice new skills on their writing, not on worksheets.	Student writing folders have become individualized and differentiated practice pads. I spiral the traits and their key qualities in my teaching over the year. I make sure students work with all the modes during the year and try new formats for writing. We use a rich variety of print and nonprint resources as mentor texts.

page 1 of 3

	Writing Neophyte	Writing Dabbler	Writing Apprentice	Writing Go-Getter	Writing Guru
How Writers Learn From Others	I don't feel comfortable modeling writing for my students.	I share a few samples of writing from outside sources but not my own. Students are tentative and struggle to verbalize what they notice in the pieces other than the obvious.	I use my own writing combined with outside sources to model how to revise and edit. Students understand but are uncertain how to apply new ideas to their own writing.	I model writing in the traits and modes to show students how a writer thinks and works. We use a variety of outside sources for inspiration, too. Students try to apply what they've noticed to their own pieces.	I regularly write with my students. I ask for their feedback on pieces I'm developing, and their ideas really rock. I model how to think like a writer all day. We incorporate ideas for how to approach writing and clarify thinking in everything we do.
How I Energize Writers	My students only want to know what to write, how long the writing is supposed to be, and if I'm going to grade it.	Only students who are confident writers ask questions. Students do what they are asked but not much more.	Students ask for help and try to use resources available in the classroom. They need coaxing, however, to revise and edit for more than obvious problems.	Students willingly engage in lessons and activities and apply what is taught to their writing to a deeper level.	Students are eager to write and ask for more time. They create interesting and complex texts and enjoy sharing. There is a high level of energy for writing.
How I Teach the Writing Process	I tell students what to write, give them a prompt, and expect them to follow it precisely. I don't spend time helping them get started; I give them written directions to follow.	Prewriting and drafting are going okay, but the revision stage just doesn't seem to work. Many students are getting better at basic editing tasks, however. Students usually write on the same topic.	Breaking down revision using the traits, and teaching editing that way, too, is making a difference. We're experimenting with writing workshops and using the traits as focus lessons. Some students are choosing their own topics.	I've woven writing workshops, writing process, writing modes, and writing traits together. Students actively revise and edit without much prompting. You hear them talk about traits as they work pieces determined primarily on their own.	The writing process is humming along. Students are comfortable choosing their own topics and formats that are important to them. They use each other and me for feedback as they revise and edit for each trait, and the result is awesome. The traits have become the shared language of our writing classroom.

	Writing Neophyte	Writing Dabbler	Writing Apprentice	Writing Go-Getter	Writing Guru
How I Apply Trait-Based Assessment	Writing assessments make me uncomfortable. I believe writing is completely subjective, so the assessment is not reliable or accurate.	I've never scored any papers using an analytic model. I can see where the trait method might be better than what I'm doing now, however.	I've practiced assessing model papers, and I'm ready to try the traits to assess papers from my own class.	I regularly use the trait scoring guide to assess student papers for one or more traits. I'm ready to try letting students assess model papers, too.	I've done so much work assessing writing with the traits that I dream of finding that perfect 6 while I sleep. My students can easily spot strengths and weaknesses in writing based on the traits. They use their Student-Friendly Guides with ease.
How I Utilize the Modes	Modes? Sounds like math.	Modes are purposes for writing. I realize I focus on one purpose more than others.	I'm gathering materials to teach the different modes and planning projects that students can do to create pieces in each mode.	I've found examples of modes in mentor texts and to model strong writing in narrative, informational/ explanatory, and argument pieces.	My students mix modes to make their writing stand out for one particular purpose. They notice how authors work with modes in the texts they read for class and for pleasure.
How I Incorporate the Standards	I'm not aware of the standards that apply to writing.	I've received basic information about the Writing standards, but they are not part of my lesson design.	I'm beginning to use the standards as a guide for lesson and project development. I'm unaware of what other teachers are doing with them for writing in my building, however.	The standards are central to my lesson planning in writing. I'm working with colleagues to coordinate and get consistency as we apply them. We're having conversations about how to maximize writing in every subject to meet the standards.	I fully integrate the Writing standards in my lessons and projects. My colleagues and I regularly meet to share ideas to meet and exceed the Writing standards. Content writing has become a central part of how my students write for many purposes and to show what they have learned.

Teaching Writing Agreement

Teacher's Name _____ Today's Date _____

Teaching Assignment _____ School Year _____

Supervisor/Evaluator _____

My score on the Writing Teacher's Self-Assessment is now _____.

Next year, I want to tackle _____.

A strength I have in teaching writing is:
(Use the Writing Teacher's Self-Assessment for reference.)

An area I'd like to improve is:
(Use the Writing Teacher's Self-Assessment for reference.)

How I plan to gain skills and confidence in this area:
(Check two to three choices.)

- ☐ Utilizing professional development on a specific writing-related topic
- ☐ Observing another teacher teaching writing
- ☐ Aligning grade-level curriculum in writing to the Common Core State Standards
- ☐ Working with a colleague to integrate new resources into instructional units
- ☐ Finding print and nonprint resource materials as mentor texts
- ☐ Taking online classes or classes from a local college or university
- ☐ Team teaching with a literacy coach on a lesson or two
- ☐ Learning how to apply technology to the writing classroom
- ☐ Visiting another school that has experienced success with writing
- ☐ Developing writing lessons and activities with grade-level teammates
- ☐ Using the school website to publish student writing
- ☐ Other _____

Supervisor/evaluator agrees to _____

_____

Teacher Signature _____ Date _____

Supervisor/Evaluator Signature:_____ Date _____

Where Writers Thrive Checklist

☐ All students are seen as, treated as, and valued as writers regardless of their skill and ability.

☐ Flip charts and key resources are posted and easy to follow.

☐ There is a happy, busy hum in the writing classroom. It is neither silent nor loud. It's "just right," so students can work independently but are comfortable checking with each other as questions arise.

☐ Oral language is prevalent throughout the day. Teachers speak carefully and use Standard English. They encourage students to do the same, correcting gently as needed. Read-alouds are a key part of the day and are selected from a variety of sources.

☐ The classroom is organized, and it's easy for students to find resources.

☐ There is an air of playfulness and engagement with—and curiosity about—language.

☐ There is ample time for teaching and practicing writing: an average of forty minutes a day.

☐ Students are cooperative and supportive of their own and classmates' writing efforts.

☐ The teacher is enthusiastic and is a learner him- or herself every day.

What Teachers and Students Need Checklist

☐ Worksheets have been replaced by writing folders that students use to practice their own writing as they learn new skills.

☐ The teacher uses reading to inspire writing in all modes and for every key quality of each trait. He or she points out the trait or key quality of the trait as the passage is read.

☐ The teacher enjoys sharing a rich variety of reading passages and using them as mentor texts, including everyday texts such as brochures, advertisements, blogs, song lyrics, and so on.

☐ Students have paper, pens, and pencils and access to computers, iPads, document cameras, and interactive whiteboards as needed.

☐ A writing center gives students access to resources. Students regularly use digital resources and have access to technology for writing time.

☐ Resources that support English learners are readily available.

☐ Anchor charts and student-generated bulletin boards and signs provide useful resource materials for students as they write.

How Writing Teachers Teach Checklist

☐ The teacher's knowledge in the area of writing is evident throughout the classroom. When working with students, he or she uses language about writing that is consistent, specific, and clear.

☐ There is evidence of the release of responsibility: gradually, students learn to work independently on writing skills—and large-group, small-group, and individual instruction are evident across a week's instruction.

☐ The teacher keeps lessons narrowed and focused. Organization and preparation are evident in the teacher's lessons and use of time, and the goal of each lesson is understood by students.

☐ The writing classroom is organized into a writing workshop format: focus lesson, guided writing, and independent writing.

☐ Not every writing lesson is conducted by sitting and writing; some require moving, art, drama, singing, and dancing. The teacher knows it's time to change things up by doing something more physical if students become restless.

☐ Students are not all at the same place in their writing. There is evidence of their working through the writing process at different stages at different times.

☐ The key qualities of the traits guide the revision and editing instruction in the classroom.

☐ The modes are used to help students decide what to write: narrative, informational/ explanatory, or argument.

How Writers Learn From Others Checklist

☐ The teacher models writing with the traits. Modeling should be age-appropriate. Modeling might also consist of a comparison to provide clarity. For instance, if the teacher is focusing on establishing voice, he or she might show the difference between: "My bike is red. My bike is fast." and "My bike is red, has six speeds, and can go so fast that I almost feel like I'm flying!"

☐ Student writing examples are shared with the class. For example, the teacher says, "We've been talking about using good word choice in our writing. As I've worked with you today, I noticed some fabulous word choice in your writing! _____, will you read how you described your dog? I love the word you used that tells your reader that you have a very big dog!"

☐ The teacher models behaviors to help students work independently. For example, the teacher asks his class, "What can you do if you're not sure how to spell a word when I'm working with a student or a group of students?" Then he models how this looks in action.

☐ The teacher models writing throughout the day and points it out to students, sometimes in a subtle manner. It may be through making a list, writing a note to a parent or another teacher, and so on.

☐ Students frequently turn to each other and read their work aloud, listening for problems in, for example, how clear the idea is or how the text sounds and getting sound, constructive advice from the listener.

How Writers Get Energized Checklist

☐ Students are engaged in the lesson and in their learning as shown through their body language, questions, interactions with each other, and ability to stay on task.

☐ Finished writing is displayed in the classroom, in the hallway, and in prominent places around the school.

☐ Students are active participants in the decisions about their writing and make appropriate choices about the tasks and efficient use of their time.

☐ Students use each other as resources.

☐ Students volunteer to share during group writing conversations.

☐ Visitors to the classroom don't distract students when they are writing. Students eagerly share what they are working on.

☐ When students finish working, they easily transition to the next task or activity.

☐ Students ask for help to clarify, provide examples, and fix mistakes. They participate fully in the lessons and activities.

☐ Students are given choices about topics and tasks.

☐ Students own their writing. It is up to them to decide to implement any guidance the teacher or their peers offer.

☐ The teacher weaves in research prompts such as, "Hmmm . . . where would we look to find that out?" as a routine part of instruction.

☐ Students ask questions about what they know and don't know and willingly seek information from multiple sources to find out what's needed.

Writing Process Checklist

☐ Students understand that writing is a process that always improves with further work. They actively seek ideas that strengthen their pieces.

☐ Different steps in the writing process are addressed using the terms *revision* and *editing* and linked to the traits.

☐ Ideas for prewriting and drafting are clearly posted for students to use as resources.

☐ Revision is modeled using the interactive whiteboard, the document camera, and someone else's writing. Students interact with the revision and then try something small from their own writing.

☐ Teachers confer with students to help during the revision and editing stages. They are selective and note one or two changes to be made. Editing is referred to as the cleanup stage of the writing process and is not focused on until students have a piece ready to share.

☐ Not every piece of writing is taken all the way through the writing process. Only significant pieces developed over time during each grading period are taken to the publication stage.

☐ A "No Excuses" or "I Can" list of common conventions is posted and adhered to in every classroom.

☐ Students know how to use resources and apply different techniques for spelling.

☐ Conventions are taught in the context of the student's own writing or in modeled pieces provided by the teacher.

☐ Students help each other as they identify editing needs in their pieces.

☐ Conventions are taught as editing skills.

The Traits of Writing Checklist

☐ The traits are used to assess student writing using the Teacher-Friendly Scoring Guides. The teacher chooses whether to use all of the traits or one or two, based on the instruction that accompanies the writing.

☐ Students regularly assess writing using their Student-Friendly Scoring Guides (pages 58–78) and discuss the strengths and weaknesses in the models based on the traits.

☐ Students use the trait language every day as they read and write.

☐ The key qualities of each trait guide the instructional component of the writing class. Evidence of the key quality in focus for the week is clearly posted and permeates the talking and thinking taking place about writing.

☐ The teacher uses trait language to confer with students individually and in small groups.

☐ Trait language is used throughout the day and across content areas. The traits are pointed out when used in a science, social studies, or math journal entry, as well as during writing workshops.

☐ The teacher keeps samples of scored student work throughout the year to document the writing progress.

☐ Formative assessment is used to guide instruction—both informal and formal writing assessments, and the teacher keeps records of every writer's strengths and areas of greatest need.

☐ Individual student needs are assessed, addressed, and handled appropriately: English learners, students with special needs, students who are talented and gifted, and so on.

Writing Modes and Purposes Checklist

☐ Evidence of writing in all modes (narrative, informational/explanatory, and argument) and in various formats is seen in the room or in the teaching.

☐ Students work on mode-specific projects that last for a significant period of time: at least one week for grades K–2 and three weeks for grades 3–8.

☐ The topics for the mode-specific papers are self-selected by students to create ownership.

☐ Students write and apply a variety of text types in their mode-specific projects.

☐ Posters and charts are used to support student writing in each mode.

☐ As texts from reading and other content areas are shared, students and the teacher note how the purpose for the piece is made clear through the writer's use of the mode.

Progress and Grades Checklist

☐ Parents are informed about the writing taking place in the classroom and ways they can support their student writers.

☐ Parents are given a copy of the Student-Friendly Scoring Guide their child will be using and are encouraged to go over it with the writing that students do at home.

☐ Student-written newsletters showcase the tasks students are working on and their progress in writing.

☐ Websites for the classroom or school post examples of student work.

☐ Before the writing is final, students are given opportunities to improve work based on conferences and other interactions. Even after initial assessments, students are encouraged to keep working if they want to improve their scores.

☐ Final grades or reports are based on what students know, what they have learned, and how close they are to meeting and exceeding Writing standards.

SIX

KNOWING THE WRITING PROGRAM IS WORKING

I want to hear that writing is taking place. Students should be sharing and talking about their writing, debating and defending their writing. Feedback should be constant, focused, and timely from both student and teacher. I know I'm seeing effective writing instruction when I see teachers modeling the writing process right in front of their students' very eyes, complete with pauses, hesitations, scratch outs, rewrites, edits, and revisions.

—Rhett Boudreau, Assistant Principal, Mountain View
Middle School, Beaverton, Oregon

There are many clues that your writing program is healthy and thriving, and few have to do with test scores. Let's be honest—higher test scores are one goal of improving the writing program, but there's a lot more to it than that. Although higher scores are an immediate payback, they are only a short-term objective. We want students to write better for any and all purposes *for the rest of their lives*, plain and simple. They need to be good writers regardless of where they go and what they do. As the administrator of the school, you owe them the best opportunities to get them ready as writers and thinkers.

So, whether your school is well on its way to being a place where writing is a top priority for every teacher—including all the content teachers and specialists—or your school is about to embark on this adventure, here are signs that the hard work going into this critical area is paying off:

- Student work is posted prominently in the hallways and on the school website.

- Examples of creative and fun writing pop up everywhere.

- Teachers are working together to write lessons that use writing in new, challenging formats.

- Writing is taking place using all different forms of technology.

- Conversations about writing happen all day long in and out of classrooms.

- Too-quiet writing classrooms are now buzzing with excitement.

- Teachers are asking you for far more resources to teach writing than the budget will allow. (Get creative: Write some grants, tap into the Parent Teacher Organization, partner with a local business, and so on.)

- Students send you samples of their writing or stop you in the hallway to listen to their work.

- Parents comment that their children have never been this excited by writing before, and they are supportive of the changes occurring in writing instruction.

- Oh yeah—test scores improve. Let's not forget that!

Top Ten Ways to Keep Writing Alive and Thriving in Your School

It's not easy turning a school into a dreamland for writing. But it can be done, one day at a time. Your leadership in this effort is critical. Without you firmly and consistently behind teachers as they strive to change their practices, it won't happen. There is no one more important than you, the school administrator, to lead the way. So, here are ten ideas to help you sustain your efforts throughout the year:

1. Begin every staff meeting with a student paper that teachers score and assess using the traits. Quickly discuss: Which traits are strong? Which traits need work? How might the teacher respond to support and encourage the writer further?

2. Recommend that a piece of writing from every student be on display at all times—in the classroom, school hallway, auditorium—anywhere in the building where it will be noticed. Tell teachers that each displayed writing sample should be as cleanly edited as possible for public view.

3. Establish a tab on the building website for publication of student writing by grade. Use software that allows students to publish their writing and receive comments from readers. Establish rules for who can view and what comprises acceptable comments.

4. Share a story or informational topic that you are interested in with students and discuss how you might write about it. Come back with a draft, invite feedback, revise, and then share your finished piece. Be honest with students about what you learned—what was easy, what was hard—and about the process you used to write.

5. Plan a schoolwide writing day. Have students pick a song about writing—or change a song's lyrics to make it about writing—and invite students to perform the songs for

other classes using simple choreography. Video the performances, and post them on the school website.

6. Arrange for older students to become writing mentors for younger students. Encourage students to collaborate and share their writing with other classmates.

7. Invite students to help write and deliver the morning announcements. Encourage them to rewrite the information with voice so it can be delivered enthusiastically and draw everyone's attention.

8. Advertise. Inform parents and the community about the writing occurring in content-area classes on the announcement board outside the school for anyone driving by to see:

   - "Science students write lab reports."

   - "Health and PE classes chart and describe fitness progress."

   - "Math students explain how to do algebra."

   - "Social studies classes write reports and create PowerPoint presentations on topics such as the lost city of Atlantis."

9. Set up a writing night for parents at the school. Assign each classroom a trait, and ask students to prepare a lively, one-minute informational presentation on that trait. Create writing passports with a place to stamp each trait, and give them to parents as they enter the school. Tell them to visit classrooms, watch the presentations, get a stamp for each trait on their passport, and then report to a common area for discussion about how they can help their young writers at home.

10. Embrace technology. Create a large poster or butcher paper sheet titled "Ways We Write Using Technology," and put it in a common area so students can add ideas over time. Begin with ideas such as "I use my iPad to take notes," or "I text my friends with my cell phone." Fill it up!

Final Thoughts

So, dear principal, administrator, teacher-leader, or whatever your job title may be, you can do this. You can make your school the writing place that turns disbelievers into avid writing teachers who will, in turn, change the writing lives of students forever. I believe that. I hope you do, too. Perhaps the ideas in this book will make your job a little easier on this front. That is my fondest wish for you—that you take this book and its resources and tackle the critical work of supporting teachers as they work with student writers. It couldn't be a more important task, and it couldn't be happening at a more important time in the literacy lives of educators.

GLOSSARY

Here are some commonly used terms in the writing classroom with quick, user-friendly definitions.

Assessment

Assessments are defined according to when they are given and what their purpose is.

- **Formative assessment:** What happens in the classroom through observation, conversation, and trait-based assessment of writing that informs the teacher about what students know and what they need to work on next

- **Interim assessment:** What happens at intervals during the year to check that students are on track to meet grade-level standards and goals

- **Summative assessment:** What happens at the end of an instructional unit or grade that provides the teacher with information about what students learned over a specific period of time

Common Core State Standards

The Common Core State Standards define what students should know and be able to do at benchmark times in their learning. In the Writing strand, there are four domains.

1. **Text Types and Purposes:** Narrative, informational/explanatory, and argument in diverse print and electronic formats (In Common Core terms, these are narrative, informational, and opinion/argument, respectively.)

2. **Production and Distribution of Writing:** The writing process (prewriting, drafting, sharing and feedback, revising, editing, and finishing or publishing) and traits (ideas, organization, voice, word choice, sentence fluency, conventions, and presentation)

3. **Research to Build and Present Knowledge:** Writing in all modes and across the content areas that requires acquisition of information from print and electronic resources, synthesis, and written interpretation of what was learned

4. **Range of Writing:** Short, midrange, and long-term assignments and projects for many different purposes in a variety of formats

Genre

Genres are categories for writing and reading. There are multiple writing subgenres within fiction, nonfiction, and poetry.

- **Fiction:** Writing that tells a story from the author's imagination; can be realistic, historical fiction, fantasy, fables, folktales, drama, mystery, humor, science fiction, tall tales, and so on

- **Nonfiction:** Writing that provides information; includes biography, autobiography, essays, history and social science, and so on

- **Poetry:** Writing that creates an emotional response through meaning, sound, rhythm, or beauty of expression; includes rhymed verse, sonnets, limericks, and so on

Modes

The **narrative** writer's purpose is to tell a story. The narrative writer typically:

- Offers a clear, well-developed story line

- Includes characters that grow and change over time

- Conveys time and setting effectively

- Presents a conflict and resolution

- Surprises, challenges, and/or entertains the reader

The **informational/explanatory** writer's purpose is to inform or explain. This writer typically:

- Informs the reader about the topic

- Transcends the obvious by explaining something interesting or curious about the topic

- Focuses on making the topic clear for the reader

- Anticipates and answers the reader's questions

- Includes details that add information, support key ideas, and help the reader make personal connections

The **argument** writer's purpose is to construct an argument. This writer typically:

- States a position clearly and sticks with it

- Offers good, sound reasoning

- Provides solid facts, opinions, and examples

- Reveals weaknesses in other positions
- Uses voice to add credibility and show confidence

Organizers and Systems

These terms refer to organizers and systems that provide easy access to student writing.

- **Writing folders:** A simple management system comprised of a folder with samples of student writing that are used as individualized practice pads for new writing skills

- **Writing portfolios:** A system to keep track of student writing progress over time; writing portfolios are typically maintained by the teacher and passed on from year to year

- **Writing notebooks:** A place where students record thoughts, words, interests, lists, questions, and information that might be useful in their writing

- **Writing journals:** A place where students return frequently and practice writing for an extended period of time to build fluency and writing stamina

Professional Learning Community

A professional learning community (PLC) is an ongoing process in which educators work collaboratively in recurring cycles of collective inquiry and action research to achieve better results for the students they serve. Professional learning communities operate under the assumption that the key to improved learning for students is continuous job-embedded learning for educators.

Rubric

A rubric is often a table that organizes the criteria used to score large-scale assessments. Rubrics usually consist of several traits or qualities and are holistically scored on a 1–4 or 1–6 scale.

Scoring Guide

A scoring guide lists the assessment criteria used at the classroom level to provide feedback to students on how their work is progressing. Scoring guides often have numerous traits or qualities and are scored analytically on a scale from 1–6.

Text Structures or Formats

Writers apply various text structures as they explore the different formats for writing. Many formats are traditional (stories, essays), and some are fresh and contemporary (blogs, marketing brochures). Text structures or formats also include different organizing structures for writing, such as comparison, contrast, point-by-point analysis, and deductive logic.

Traits of Writing

The "traits of writing" is the common language used to assess and teach writing. It is sometimes referred to as 6+1 because there are six core traits plus one (presentation) that is a small motor and visual skill; together, they represent the range of skills needed in strong presentation pieces of writing.

1. **Ideas:** The piece's content—its central message and the details that support that message

2. **Organization:** The internal structure of the piece—the thread of logic and the pattern of meaning

3. **Voice:** The tone and tenor of the piece—the personal stamp of the writer, which is achieved through a strong understanding of purpose and audience

4. **Word choice:** The specific vocabulary the writer uses to convey meaning and enlighten the reader

5. **Sentence fluency:** The way words and phrases flow through the piece—the auditory trait, because it's "read" with the ear as much as the eye

6. **Conventions:** The mechanical correctness of the piece—correct use of conventions (spelling, capitalization, punctuation, paragraphing, and grammar and usage) guides the reader through the text easily

7. **Presentation:** The physical appearance of the piece—a visually appealing text provides a welcome mat and invites the reader in

For each trait, four content subjects are used to assess and teach writing:

1. **Ideas**

    a. Finding a topic

    b. Focusing the topic

    c. Developing the topic

    d. Using details

2. **Organization**

    a. Creating the lead

    b. Using sequence words and transition words

    c. Structuring the body

    d. Ending with a sense of resolution

3. **Voice**

    a. Establishing a tone

    b. Conveying the purpose

    c. Creating a connection to the audience

    d. Taking risks to create voice

4. **Word Choice**

    a. Applying strong verbs

    b. Selecting striking words and phrases

    c. Using specific and accurate words

    d. Choosing words that deepen meaning

5. **Sentence Fluency**

    a. Crafting well-built sentences

    b. Varying sentence types

    c. Capturing smooth and rhythmic flow

    d. Breaking the rules to create fluency

6. **Conventions**

    a. Checking spelling

    b. Punctuating effectively and paragraphing accurately

    c. Capitalizing correctly

    d. Applying grammar and usage

7. **Presentation**

    a. Applying handwriting skills

    b. Using word processing effectively

    c. Making good use of white space

    d. Refining text features

Writing Process

This process consists of the recursive steps writers go through to generate text. Although listed in a specific order, it's possible and even likely that writers will move through the writing process in the order that makes the best sense for their writing.

1. **Prewriting:** Selecting a topic, gathering information, choosing a text type, and planning the draft

2. **Drafting:** Getting the ideas down in an early form that can be very rough

3. **Sharing and feedback:** Thinking about how clear the writing is in the draft; the writer and reader communicate in writing or in a conference about ideas to improve the piece.

4. **Revising:** Changing the draft based on the ideas from sharing and feedback; the writer incorporates new ideas to make the writing idea as clear as possible by applying the ideas, organization, voice, word choice, and sentence fluency traits.

5. **Editing:** Cleaning up the copy so it is easy for the reader to read; the writer incorporates what he or she knows about conventions by checking spelling, capitalization, punctuation, grammar and usage, and paragraph breaks.

6. **Finishing or publishing:** Creating a final copy and taking it public

REFERENCES AND RESOURCES

Applebee, A. N. (1986). Problems in process approaches: Toward a reconceptualization of process instruction. In A. R. Petrosky & D. Bartholomae (Eds.), *The teaching of writing, part II: Eighty-fifth yearbook of the National Society for the Study of Education* (pp. 95–113). Chicago: National Society for the Study of Education.

Applebee, A. N. (2003). Balancing the curriculum in the English language arts: Exploring the components of effective teaching and learning. In J. Flood, D. Lapp, J. R. Squire, & J. M. Jensen (Eds.), *Handbook of research on teaching the English language arts* (2nd ed., pp. 676–684). Mahwah, NJ: Erlbaum.

Applebee, A. N., Langer, J. A., Nystrand, M., & Gamoran, A. (2003). Discussion-based approaches to developing understanding: Classroom instruction and student performance in middle and high school English. *American Educational Research Journal, 40*(3), 685–730.

Arter, J., Spandel, V., Culham, R., & Pollard, J. (1994). *Study findings on the integration of writing assessment & instruction: School centers for classroom assessment final report, 1992–93.* Portland, OR: Northwest Regional Educational Laboratory.

Atwell, N. (1987). *In the middle: New understandings about writing, reading, and learning.* Portsmouth, NH: Boynton/Cook.

Beers, K., Probst, R., & Rief, L. (Eds.). (2007). *Adolescent literacy: Turning promise into practice.* Portsmouth, NH: Heinemann.

Braddock, R., Lloyd-Jones, R., & Schoer, L. (1963). *Research in written composition.* Champaign, IL: National Council of Teachers of English.

Brenner, D., Pearson, P. D., & Rief, L. (2007). Thinking through assessment. In K. Beers, R. E. Probst, & L. Rief (Eds.), *Adolescent literacy: Turning promise into practice* (pp. 257–272). Portsmouth, NH: Heinemann.

Brookhart, S. M., & Moss, C. M. (2013). Leading by learning. *Phi Delta Kappan, 94*(8), 13.

Calkins, L. M. (1986). *The art of teaching writing.* Portsmouth, NH: Heinemann.

Calkins, L. M. (1994). *The art of teaching writing* (New ed.). Portsmouth, NH: Heinemann.

Cazden, C. B. (1979). Peekaboo as an instructional model: Discourse development in home and at school. *Papers and Reports on Child Language Development* (No. 17). Stanford: Stanford University Department of Linguistics.

Center for the Education and Study of Diverse Populations. (2013). *Application of the Common Core State Standards for students in special education.* Accessed at www.cesdp.nmhu.edu/ccss /application-of-ccss-for-students-in-special-education.html on September 3, 2013.

Cramer, R. L. (2001). *Creative power: The nature and nurture of children's writing.* New York: Longman.

DeFoe, M. C. (2000). *Using directed writing strategies to teach students writing skills in middle grades language arts.* Fort Lauderdale, FL: Nova Southeastern University. (ERIC Document Reproduction Service No. ED444186)

Emig, J. A. (1971). *The composing processes of twelfth graders.* Urbana, IL: National Council of Teachers of English.

Escribano, P. D. (1999). Teaching writing through reading: A text-centered approach. *Ibérica, 1,* 55–62. Accessed at www.aelfe.org/documents/text1-Duran.pdf on April 13, 2012.

Fletcher, R. (1992). *What a writer needs.* Portsmouth, NH: Heinemann.

Gallagher, C. W., & Lee, A. (2008). *Teaching writing that matters: Tools and projects that motivate adolescent writers.* New York: Scholastic.

Garrison, C., & Ehringhaus, M. (2007). *Formative and summative assessments in the classroom.* Accessed at www.amle.org/publications/webexclusive/assessment/tabid/1120/default.aspx on May 17, 2013.

Gilbert, J., & Graham, S. (2010). Teaching writing to elementary students in grades 4 to 6: A national survey. *The Elementary School Journal, 110*(4), 494–518.

Graham, S., Harris, K., & Hebert, M. (2011). *Informing writing: The benefits of formative assessment—A report from Carnegie Corporation of New York.* Washington, DC: Alliance for Excellent Education.

Graham, S., & Hebert, M. (2010). *Writing to read: Evidence for how writing can improve reading—A report from Carnegie Corporation of New York.* Washington, DC: Alliance for Excellent Education.

Graham, S., & Perin, D. (2007). *Writing next: Effective strategies to improve writing of adolescents in middle and high schools—A report to Carnegie Corporation of New York.* Washington, DC: Alliance for Excellent Education.

Graves, D. H. (1983). *Writing: Teachers and children at work.* Exeter, NH: Heinemann.

Graves, D. H. (1994). *A fresh look at writing.* Portsmouth, NH: Heinemann.

Hall, D., & Emblen, D. L. (Eds.). (1994). *A writer's reader* (7th ed.). New York: HarperCollins College.

Hall, D., & Emblen, D. L. (Eds.). (2001). *A writer's reader* (9th ed.). New York: Longman.

Hillocks, G., Jr. (1986). *Research on written composition: New directions for teaching.* Urbana, IL: National Council of Teachers of English.

Hillocks, G., Jr. (2002). *The testing trap: How state writing assessments control learning.* New York: Teachers College Press.

International Reading Association & National Council of Teachers of English. (1996). *Standards for the English language arts.* Newark, DE: Authors.

Krashen, S., & Lee, S.-Y. (2004). Competence in foreign language writing: Progress and lacunae. *Literacy Across Cultures, 12*(2), 10–14.

Langer, J. A., & Applebee, A. N. (1986). Reading and writing instruction: Toward a theory of teaching and learning. *Review of Research in Education, 13*, 171–194.

Lee, S.-Y., & Krashen, S. (2002). Predictors of success in writing in English as a foreign language: Reading, revision behavior, apprehension, and writing. *College Student Journal, 36*(4), 532–543.

Lenhart, A., Arafeh, S., Smith, A., & Macgill, A. R. (2008). *Writing, technology and teens.* Washington, DC: Pew Internet and American Life Project.

Litwin, E. (2010). *Pete the cat: I love my white shoes.* New York: HarperCollins.

Murray, D. M. (1985). *A writer teaches writing* (2nd ed.). Boston: Houghton Mifflin.

National Center for Education Statistics. (2007). *The nation's report card: Writing 2007* (NCES 2008–468). Accessed at http://nces.ed.gov/nationsreportcard/pdf/main2007/2008468.pdf on April 13, 2012.

National Center for Education Statistics. (2012). *The nation's report card: Writing 2011* (NCES 2012–470). Washington, DC: Author.

National Commission on Writing in America's Schools and Colleges. (2003). *The neglected "R": The need for a writing revolution.* Accessed at www.host-collegeboard.com/advocacy/writing/publications.html on May 20, 2013.

National Council of Teachers of English. (2008). *Writing now: A policy research brief.* Urbana, IL: Author.

National Governors Association for Best Practices & Council of Chief State School Officers. (n.d.a). *Application of Common Core State Standards for English language learners.* Accessed at www.corestandards.org/assets/application-for-english-learners.pdf on May 20, 2013.

National Governors Association Center for Best Practices and Council of Chief State School Officers. (n.d.b). *Application to students with disabilities.* Accessed at www.corestandards.org/assets/application-to-students-with-disabilities.pdf on May 20, 2013.

National Governors Association Center for Best Practices & Council of Chief State School Officers. (2010). *Common Core State Standards for English language arts & literacy in history/social studies, science, and technical subjects.* Washington, DC: Authors.

National Writing Project & Nagin, C. (2003). *Because writing matters: Improving student writing in our schools.* San Francisco: Jossey-Bass.

Perl, S. (1979). The composing processes of unskilled college writers. *Research in the Teaching of English, 13*(4), 317–336.

Prensky, M. (2012). *From digital natives to digital wisdom: Hopeful essays for 21st century learning.* Thousand Oaks, CA: Corwin Press.

Prior, P. (2006). A sociocultural theory of writing. In C. A. MacArthur, S. Graham, & J. Fitzgerald (Eds.), *Handbook of writing research* (pp. 54–66). New York: Guilford Press.

Pritchard, R. J., & Honeycutt, R. L. (2006). The process approach to writing instruction: Examining its effectiveness. In C. A. MacArthur, S. Graham, & J. Fitzgerald (Eds.), *Handbook of writing research* (pp. 275–290). New York: Guilford Press.

Scholastic & Bill and Melinda Gates Foundation. (2012). *Primary sources: 2012—America's teachers on the teaching profession.* New York: Scholastic.

Smarter Balanced Assessment Consortium. (2012). *Smarter Balanced Assessment Consortium: English language arts item and task specifications.* Washington, DC: Author.

Thomason, T., & York, C. (2000). *Write on target: Preparing young writers to succeed on state writing achievement tests.* Norwood, MA: Christopher-Gordon.

Wood, D. J., Bruner, J. S., & Ross, G. (1976). The role of tutoring in problem solving. *Journal of Child Psychiatry and Psychology, 17*(2), 89–100.

INDEX

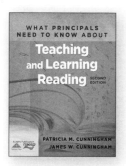

What Principals Need to Know About Teaching and Learning Reading, 2nd Edition
Patricia M. Cunningham and James W. Cunningham
Principals will discover strategies for improving reading programs using the foundation established by the six truths of reading instruction. Explore comprehensive techniques, troubleshoot problems your teachers may face, and gain valuable approaches to topics such as reading comprehension, vocabulary and literacy, and phonics and fluency.
BKF563

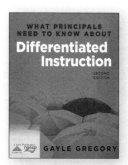

What Principals Need to Know About Differentiated Instruction, 2nd Edition
Gayle Gregory
This valuable resource gives administrators the knowledge and skills needed to enable teachers to implement and sustain differentiation. Learn information and strategies to jump-start, guide, and coach teachers as they respond to the needs of diverse students.
BKF536

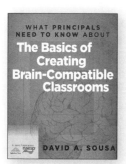

What Principals Need to Know About the Basics of Creating Brain-Compatible Classrooms
David A. Sousa
Understand the basics for creating a brain-compatible classroom with this brief, accessible guide customized for principals. This book provides an overview of educational neuroscience designed to help principals construct meaningful professional development that enhances teachers' knowledge and skills about brain-compatible learning.
BKF463

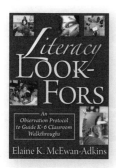

Literacy Look-Fors
Elaine K. McEwan-Adkins
Understand the indicators of effective literacy instruction, and learn how to identify the look-fors. Literacy leaders will gain the power to bring all students to grade level, or well above, when it comes to literacy attainment.
BKF422

Common Core English Language Arts in a PLC at Work™, Leader's Guide
Douglas Fisher, Nancy Frey, and Cynthia L. Uline
Integrate the CCSS for English language arts into your school's instruction, curriculum, assessment, and intervention practices with this straightforward resource. Using specific leader-driven examples and scenarios, discover the what and how of teaching so you can ensure students master the standards.
BKF578

Solution Tree | Press   *a division of* Solution Tree   Visit solution-tree.com or call 800.733.6786 to order.

Wait! Your professional development journey doesn't have to end with the last pages of this book.

We realize improving student learning doesn't happen overnight. And your school or district shouldn't be left to puzzle out all the details of this process alone.

No matter where you are on the journey, we're committed to helping you get to the next stage.

Take advantage of everything from **custom workshops** to **keynote presentations** and **interactive web and video conferencing**. We can even help you develop an action plan tailored to fit your specific needs.

Let's get the conversation started.

Call 888.763.9045 today.

 solution-tree.com

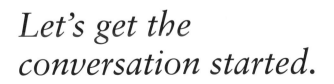

Solution Tree

Solution Tree's mission is to advance the work of our authors. By working with the best researchers and educators worldwide, we strive to be the premier provider of innovative publishing, in-demand events, and inspired professional development designed to transform education to ensure that all students learn.

The mission of the National Association of Elementary School Principals is to lead in the advocacy and support for elementary and middle level principals and other education leaders in their commitment for all children.

◧ SCHOLASTIC

The corporate mission of Scholastic is to encourage the intellectual and personal growth of all children, beginning with literacy, the cornerstone of all learning. With more than 90 years of experience supporting the learning lives of children, today Scholastic remains committed to providing quality, engaging educational content in digital and print formats for the next generation of learners, and the families and educators who guide them.